MY FIRST BRITANNICA

Physical Sciences
and Technology

2

ENCYCLOPÆDIA
Britannica®

CHICAGO   LONDON   NEW DELHI   PARIS   SEOUL   SYDNEY   TAIPEI   TOKYO

© 2004 by Encyclopædia Britannica, Inc.

International Standard Book Number: 1-59339-048-3 (set)
International Standard Book Number: 1-59339-050-5 (volume 2)

My First Britannica:
Volume 2: Physical Sciences and Technology 2004

Britannica.com may be accessed on the Internet at http://www.britannica.com.

Encyclopædia Britannica, Britannica, and the Thistle logo are registered trademarks of Encyclopædia Britannica, Inc.

Physical Sciences and Technology

TABLE OF CONTENTS

Milky Way Galaxy
© Myron Jay Dorf/Corbis

Physical Sciences and Technology

INTRODUCTION

**Where does medicine come from? What was Gutenberg's gift?
Are aliens waiting for us in outer space?
Can eyes ever hear?**

In Volume 2, *Physical Sciences and Technology,* you'll discover answers to these questions and many more. Through pictures, articles, and fun facts, you'll journey through space, meet great inventors, and investigate wonderful things about the world.

To help you on your journey, we've provided the following signposts in *Physical Sciences and Technology*:

■ **Subject Tabs**—The coloured box in the upper corner of each right-hand page will quickly tell you the article subject.

■ **Search Lights**—Try these mini-quizzes before and after you read the article and see how much - *and how quickly* - you can learn. You can even make this a game with a reading partner. (Answers are upside down at the bottom of one of the pages.)

■ **Did You Know?**—Check out these fun facts about the article subject. With these surprising 'factoids', you can entertain your friends, impress your teachers, and amaze your parents.

■ **Picture Captions**—Read the captions that go with the photos. They provide useful information about the article subject.

■ **Vocabulary**—New or difficult words are in **bold type**. You'll find them explained in the Glossary at the back of this volume. And there's a complete listing of all Glossary terms in the set in the **Reference Guide and Index**, Volume 13.

■ **Learn More!**—Follow these pointers to related articles throughout the set.

And don't forget: If you're not sure where to start, where you saw something before, or where to go next, the **Reference Guide and Index** (Volume 13) will point the way.

Have a great trip!

MY FIRST BRITANNICA

SEARCH LIGHT

Which of
these things
do astronomers
study?
- stars
- planets
- moons
- astronauts
- comets

Studying the Stars

Look at the sky. What do you see?

If it's day you'll see the Sun. If it's night you'll see the Moon. And if the sky is clear you'll see stars. In big cities you may see only a few hundred stars. But out in the country or on the ocean you'll see many thousands. You may even see planets and, if you're lucky, a **comet**.

There are people who look at the sky for hours and hours, night after night. They study the stars, the planets, and other objects in the sky. These people are called 'astronomers'. The word 'astronomy' comes from the Greek for 'star' and 'arrangement'.

Astronomers study the universe in many different ways. Some watch faraway objects. Others work in **laboratories** where they look at samples of **meteorites**, rocks from the Moon, and space **debris** from other planets. Some try to make models of the different objects people have studied.

Not all astronomers get paid for the work they do. Some do it for a hobby. Such people are called 'amateur astronomers'.

How do astronomers study objects that are millions, even billions, of kilometres away? They use powerful telescopes that make things look large enough to be seen in detail. Some telescopes are small enough to be held in the hand. Others are as big as a bus!

LEARN MORE! READ THESE ARTICLES...
GALILEO (VOLUME 4) • TELESCOPES (VOLUME 2) • UNIVERSE (VOLUME 2)

Answer: They study all of these except for astronauts.

Infinite Space

The universe is a vast **expanse** of space that contains all matter and energy, from the smallest particle to the biggest galaxy. It contains all the planets, the Sun, stars, asteroids, our Milky Way galaxy, and all the other galaxies too.

No one knows how big the universe is. Astronomers believe that it is still growing outwards in every direction.

How did it all begin? No one is really sure of that either.

Most scientists believe that at first everything was one incredibly solid, heavy ball of matter. This ball exploded billions of years ago - and the universe was born. The moment of this explosion is called the 'big bang'. It is from this moment that time began.

After the explosion, the early universe was small and extremely hot. As it cooled, it expanded and pieces spread out. Small pieces formed the basic

SEARCH LIGHT

If the universe is still growing, is it moving towards or away from the Earth?

elements hydrogen and helium. Other pieces began to join together, and objects began to form. Over billions of years, the objects became galaxies, stars, and planets.

How the universe was formed is still only a theory (an idea). But different parts of it have proved to be true over the years. Astronomers continue to **investigate** the theory. One way they do this is by using a 'spectroscope'. A spectroscope measures the colour of light coming from an object. Changes in the colour indicate whether an object is moving away from or towards the Earth.

Because of spectroscope readings, scientists believe that the universe is still growing outwards in every direction.

LEARN MORE! READ THESE ARTICLES.
ATOMS (VOLUME 2) • GALAXIES (VOLUME)
SOLAR SYSTEM (VOLUME 2)

DID YOU KNOW?
Scientists believe that much of the universe may be made of something called 'dark matter'. This hidden mass may be a substance that people have never before encountered.

Answer: Everything in the universe is moving away from everything else. You can see how this works by drawing black dots on a balloon, then blowing it up and watching the dots spread apart.

Distant Fire

All stars are basically enormous balls of fire. They are made up of gases that give off both heat and light as they burn. Their power comes from nuclear energy, the same source that both powers atomic bombs and produces electricity in many parts of the world.

The life of a star spans billions of years. A star is born from clouds of dust and the **element** hydrogen. This cloud mass forms a spinning ball and becomes extremely hot. It becomes so hot that the hydrogen gas begins to glow. The glowing gas ball is called a 'protostar' ('proto' means 'beginning' or 'first').

A protostar slowly becomes bigger until eventually it stops growing. It is then a star, and it can continue to glow for millions of years. But eventually it starts to cool off. It turns red and grows larger once more. It becomes a 'red giant'. Then the star begins to die. How long a star lives depends on how big it is. The bigger the star, the longer it lives.

In large stars, the heat inside the star produces iron. This iron acts like a sponge and soaks up the star's energy. The energy eventually causes a big explosion called a 'supernova'. In some cases, what is left may become a black hole. Black holes are like giant vacuum cleaners in space that suck up everything around them, including light.

Our Sun is still a young star, although it is already billions of years old. It will be many more billions of years before it begins to die. So there's still time to finish your homework!

DID YOU KNOW?

After our own Sun, the nearest star to Earth is Alpha Proxima Centuri. It is 4.3 light-years away, or almost 1.3 billion kilometres from Earth.

SEARCH LIGHT

True or false? Black holes were once stars.

LEARN MORE! READ THESE ARTICLES...
GALAXIES (VOLUME 2) • NUCLEAR ENERGY (VOLUME 2)
UNIVERSE (VOLUME 2)

When you look up at the night sky, it's hard to believe that all those twinkling stars are actually enormous balls of fire.
© Matthias Kulka/Corbis

Answer: TRUE. Black holes are former stars that have collapsed inwards and now swallow up all material and light around them.

Star Clusters

When we look at the sky at night, we can sometimes see thousands of stars shining brightly. They look as if they have been scattered around the sky. But actually, most stars are clustered together in huge groups. These groups are called 'galaxies'.

Our Sun is part of a galaxy. It is the Milky Way Galaxy. On a very clear night, if you look carefully at the sky, you might see part of this whitish band of stars stretching from one side to the other.

The universe is so huge that the Milky Way Galaxy is only one of many galaxies. Astronomers think that there are billions of galaxies in the universe. Each of these galaxies may contain trillions of stars, many much bigger than our Sun! The Milky Way itself contains several billion stars.

Some galaxies have no regular shape. Others, like the Milky Way, are shaped a bit like a giant merry-go-round. Each one has a centre around which stars move in circles.

It is hard to see the other galaxies in the sky with the naked eye. Even though they are incredibly large, they are also incredibly far away. Scientists must use powerful telescopes to study other galaxies. For this reason it takes a long time to learn even a little bit about another galaxy. And there's still a great deal we haven't learned about our own galaxy.

SEARCH LIGHT

Find and correct the mistake in the following sentence: There are many, many universes in the galaxy.

LEARN MORE! READ THESE ARTICLES…
SOLAR SYSTEM (VOLUME 2) • TELESCOPES (VOLUME 2)
UNIVERSE (VOLUME 2)

DID YOU KNOW?
Unlike galaxies, constellations are groups of stars. People used to imagine connecting the stars to make pictures in the night sky. Most constellations are named after animals and mythological figures. They still help astronomers and navigators locate certain stars.

Our galaxy, the Milky Way, is shaped a bit like a giant merry-go-round. Its billions of stars move in circles around the centre.
© Myron Jay Dorf/Corbis

Life Beyond the Earth

Could there be life elsewhere in the universe? There are some people who think that it's possible. They have given the idea a name, extraterrestrial life. 'Extra' means 'beyond' and 'terrestrial' means 'of the Earth', so altogether the name means 'life beyond the Earth'.

Most scientists believe that for another planet to have life on it, it must have an **atmosphere** (air), light, heat, and water like the Earth does.

We get our light and heat from the Sun. The universe is filled with millions of stars like our Sun. Scientists are trying to find out if these stars have planets - perhaps Earth-like planets. If there is such a planet, then it could have life on it.

It's not easy to find extraterrestrial life. The universe is an immense place to search. Some scientists believe that if there is intelligent life elsewhere, it may send radio signals to us. So far, the only signals that scientists have found are the natural ones that come from stars and planets themselves.

SEARCH LIGHT

In addition to an atmosphere, which three things are needed for life?
a) water, heat, and air
b) dirt, heat, and light
c) water, heat, and light

Whether it is possible or not, the idea of beings on other planets has excited people for years. Some believe that aliens from other worlds have even visited Earth. They call these aliens 'extraterrestrials' or 'ETs'. Some even claim to have seen ETs and their spaceships, which are called 'unidentified flying objects' or simply 'UFOs'.

What do you think? Are there creatures living on other planets? And how do you think they would live?

LEARN MORE! READ THESE ARTICLES...
ASTRONAUTS (VOLUME 2) • SPACECRAFT (VOLUME 2) • UNIVERSE (VOLUME 2)

Exploring the New Frontier

Once, the Moon was the only important thing in **orbit** around planet Earth. Today, many objects circling the Earth have been launched into space by people. All these orbiters, including the Moon, are called '**satellites**'. Those launched by people are called '**artificial** satellites'.

Communications satellites send telephone, television, and other electronic signals to and from different places on Earth. Weather satellites take pictures of the clouds and wind systems. Various scientific satellites gather information about outer space. There are even 'spy' satellites which take pictures for the military. And there are space stations.

In the late 20th century, the United States, Russia, the European Space Agency, Japan, and Canada joined forces to build the International Space Station (the ISS). It is meant to have people on it all the time. In 1998, the first two ISS **modules** were launched and joined together in space. In November 2000, the first three-person crew, an American and two Russians, occupied the station, which was still being added to.

Large space stations are planned for the future. These will have many people working in them all the time. They could be like airports are today, where a person changes planes to go to a specific destination. But from a spaceport, people would change spacecraft to travel to the Moon, another planet, or another space station.

LEARN MORE! READ THESE ARTICLES...
MOON (VOLUME 2) • PLANETS (VOLUME 2)
SOLAR SYSTEM (VOLUME 2)

DID YOU KNOW?

In order to leave the Earth's gravity and visit a space station, you have to travel at a speed of 11 kilometres per second.

SEARCH LIGHT

Why is a space station called a satellite?

In November 2000 the first three-person crew - an American and two Russians - occupied the still-growing International Space Station.
© NASA

Going Up in Space

Space is what we call the area that's 160 kilometres or more above Earth's surface. Below that boundary is Earth's **atmosphere** - the layer of gases including the air we breathe. In space there is no air to breathe. And it is very, very cold.

Russia and the United States were the first countries to send people into space. Russia's space travellers are called 'cosmonauts', which means 'space sailors'. Those from America are called 'astronauts', meaning 'star sailors'.

In 1961 cosmonaut Yuri Gagarin became the first man to travel into space. In 1969 astronaut Neil Armstrong became the first man to walk on the Moon. Sally Ride, in 1983, was the first American woman astronaut.

Today people travel into space inside **space shuttles** that ride piggyback on a rocket into space. After blastoff, the Earth outside the shuttle moves farther and farther away until it looks like a big blue-and-white sea outside the astronauts' window.

In space anything not tied down will float - including the astronauts themselves! Earth's gravity has become too weak to hold things down. In fact, it's hard to tell what 'down' means in space.

The shuttle's many special machines help astronauts live in space. The main computer helps fly the shuttle and control conditions within it. A long metal arm lets the astronauts handle things outside their ship. And many other machines are carried along for experiments.

Today most space shuttle trips are to space stations, where astronauts and cosmonauts can live while they work in space.

LEARN MORE! READ THESE ARTICLES…
GRAVITY (VOLUME 2) • MOON (VOLUME 2)
SPACECRAFT (VOLUME 2)

> **DID YOU KNOW?**
> Because different planets have different gravities, an astronaut's weight would change from planet to planet. For example, an astronaut weighing 75 kilos on Earth would weigh only 28 kilos on Mars but 177 kilos on Jupiter.

SEARCH LIGHT

Space is the area
a) more than 160 kilometres out from Earth.
b) more than 16 kilometres out from Earth.
c) more than 16,000 kilometres out from Earth.

Imagine you are lying on your back inside a space shuttle. Two long rockets will help your heavy spaceship get off the ground. With five seconds to go, the fuel in your spaceship starts burning. 'Five…four…three…two…one'.
NASA

SEARCH LIGHT

Which of these would you *not* find in the solar system?
- galaxy
- star
- planet
- comet
- asteroid

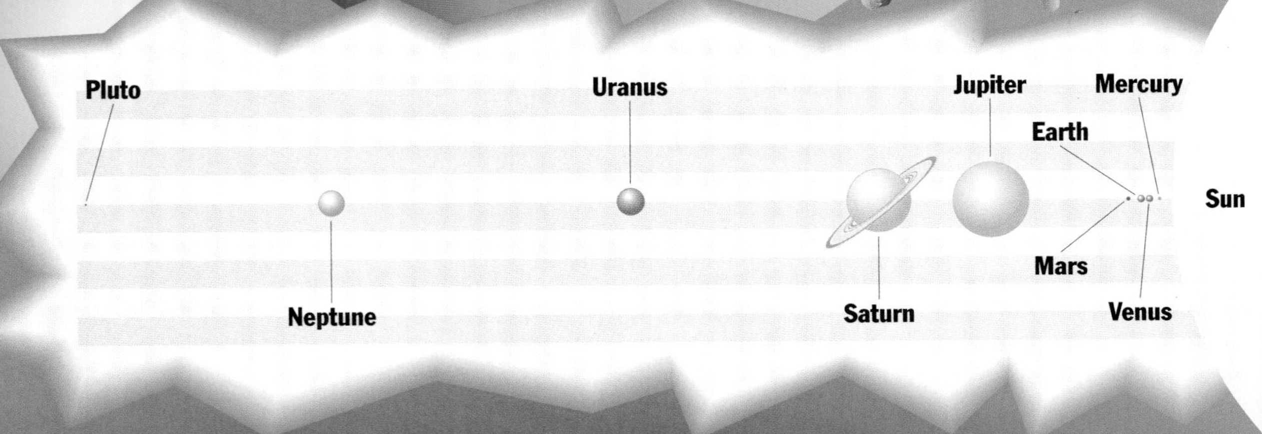

Pluto

Uranus

Jupiter

Mercury

Earth

Sun

Mars

Neptune

Saturn

Venus

Family of the Sun

Imagine a huge black space. The Sun moves through this vast space, taking many smaller bodies with it. These bodies include planets, asteroids, comets, meteors, and tiny **molecules** of gases. The Sun and its companions are known as a 'solar system'. Many solar systems and stars clustered together make up a galaxy.

Astronomers do not know how far out our solar system extends. We think that Pluto is the last planet to **orbit** the Sun, but there could still be more. At its farthest point from the Sun, Pluto is about 7.2 billion kilometres away.

The Sun provides energy for the rest of the solar system. It also provides the heat and light necessary for life on our planet. And its **gravity** keeps the planets, comets, and other bodies in orbit.

After the Sun, the planets are the largest and most **massive** members of the solar system. There are nine known planets: Mercury, Venus, Earth, Mars, Jupiter, Saturn, Uranus, Neptune, and Pluto.

Asteroids, known as 'minor planets', are smaller bodies. Most asteroids lie between Mars and Jupiter. Ceres is the largest asteroid.

A comet appears in the sky as a fuzzy spot of light with a tail streaming after it. It is made up of dust and frozen gases. As this giant dirty snowball moves closer to the Sun, the ice melts, making what looks like a tail. Halley's Comet is probably the most famous of all the comets.

LEARN MORE! READ THESE ARTICLES…
ASTEROIDS (VOLUME 2)
GALAXIES (VOLUME 2) • PLANETS • (VOLUME 2)

DID YOU KNOW?
The Sun's temperature on the surface is about 5,537 to 6,093°C. That's 100 times hotter than a really hot day on Earth!

Answer: Galaxies are made up of stars and solar systems, not the other way around.

Minor Planets

On January 1st in 1801, a man named Giuseppe Piazzi found a new object in the sky. It was circling the Sun out beyond the planet Mars, and Piazzi thought it might be a comet. Some people thought that it was a new planet. Over the next few years many more objects were seen. All of these were much smaller than a planet. Astronomers now call these objects 'asteroids' or 'minor planets'.

There are thousands of asteroids in our solar system. They tend to vary in shape, ranging from large **spheres** to smaller slabs and potato-shaped objects. Some asteroids are big. Most are the size of a boulder. The asteroid that Piazzi found, called Ceres, is the biggest discovered so far. Its **diameter** is about 930 kilometres. Smaller asteroids form when two big asteroids smash into each other and break up. Astronomers think that there are millions of tiny asteroids in the solar system.

Like planets, all asteroids in our solar system circle the Sun. The path that a planet or an asteroid follows when it circles the Sun is called an 'orbit'. Most asteroids are found farther from the Sun than Earth, between the orbits of Mars and Jupiter. Some, though, come quite close to the Sun.

Many people believe that millions of years ago an asteroid hit Earth and led to the dinosaurs' dying out. Some filmmakers in Hollywood have even made popular science-fiction films using the idea of an asteroid hitting Earth.

LEARN MORE! READ THESE ARTICLES...
DINOSAURS:
A MYSTERY DISAPPEARANCE (VOLUME 1)
PLANETS (VOLUME 2)
SOLAR SYSTEM (VOLUME 2)

SEARCH LIGHT

Fill in the gap:
An asteroid might have been involved in the disappearance of the dinosaurs when it crashed into _____.

DID YOU KNOW?

Here's a surprise: not all asteroids are in outer space! Starfish are also called asteroids. The name that these two very different things share means 'starlike'.

 Answer: An asteroid might have been involved in the disappearance of the dinosaurs when it crashed into Earth.

If Halley's
Comet came
around in 1759,
1835, 1910,
and 1986,
about how many
years does it
take to appear?

DID YOU KNOW?

American author Mark Twain,
who wrote *Tom Sawyer*, was
born in 1835 on a day when
Halley's Comet could be seen
in the sky. Just as he
predicted, he died when
Halley's Comet was again
seen in the sky, in 1910.

Rocketing Masses
with Fuzzy Tails

The word 'comet' comes from a Greek word that means 'hairy one'. A comet sometimes looks like a star with a hairy tail. But a comet is not a star. Like the Moon, a comet has no light of its own. A comet shines from the sunlight bouncing off it. Like the Earth, a comet goes around the Sun, so it may appear again and again.

But if a comet isn't a star, what is it?

Some scientists think that a large part of a comet is ice. The rest is bits of iron and dust and perhaps a few big chunks of rock. When sunshine melts the ice in a comet, great clouds of gas go streaming behind it. These clouds make the bright fuzzy-looking tail.

Long ago when there were no streetlights and the air was very clean, everyone could see comets. Unlike the stars that shone every night, comets seemed to appear quite suddenly. People thought that they would bring bad luck such as floods, hungry times, or sickness.

The English astronomer Edmond Halley, who lived over 200 years ago, discovered about 24 different comets. One that keeps coming back was named for him because he worked out when it would return. Halley first saw it in 1759, and it reappeared in 1835, 1910, and 1986. The next time it comes near the Earth will be in the year 2060.

How old will you be then?

LEARN MORE! READ THESE ARTICLES…
ASTEROIDS (VOLUME 2) • ASTRONOMY (VOLUME 2) • SOLAR SYSTEM (VOLUME 2)

Derke/O'Hara/Stone

Answer: Halley's Comet generally comes around every 76 years, though sometimes it takes just 75.

SEARCH LIGHT

Find out what you would weigh on the Moon. Take your weight and divide by 7.

A Trip to the Moon

Would you like to go to the Moon? One day you may be able to.

Astronauts have already visited the Moon. They took their own food, water, and air. You would have to take these things with you too, because the Moon doesn't have them.

Astronaut Edwin E. ('Buzz') Aldrin on 20 July 1969, one of the first two people to walk on the Moon.
NASA/JPL/Caltech

Compared with the planets, the Moon is very close to the Earth. It is only 400,000 kilometres away. Spaceships travel fast enough to cover this distance in a matter of hours.

One day there may be little towns on the Moon. The first ones will probably be covered over and filled with air. When you're inside a Moon town, you'll be able to breathe normally without a spacesuit or air tank. But you will need to wear a spacesuit and an air tank outside.

When you walk outside the Moon town, you will feel a lot lighter. You will be able to take giant steps of more than three metres. You'll be able to throw a ball almost out of sight. This is because the Moon has fairly weak gravity, the force that prevents things from flying off into space.

Gravity is also what gives your body weight. You will not weigh as much on the Moon as you do on Earth. If you weigh 20 kilos on Earth, you'll weigh only around 3 kilos on the Moon!

From the Moon you'll see many more stars than you can see from Earth. They'll also seem much brighter because you won't be looking through layers of air and pollution. And you'll be able to enjoy this view for two whole weeks at a time. That's the length of the Moon's night!

LEARN MORE! READ THESE ARTICLES...
GRAVITY (VOLUME 2) • SOLAR SYSTEM (VOLUME 2) • SPACECRAFT (VOLUME 2)

> **DID YOU KNOW?**
>
> Since there's no wind or water on the Moon, the astronauts' footprints could still be there in 10 million years.

Answer: If your Earth weight is 28 kilos, for example, your Moon weight would be only about 4 kilos.

Wanderers
in the Sky

Billions of years ago, there was an enormous swirling cloud of gas and dust. This cloud packed together and became extremely hot. Eventually, the centre of the cloud formed our Sun. The rest of the cloud clumped together until it formed planets.

The nine planets in our solar system revolve (or circle) around our Sun. Beginning with the one closest to the Sun, they are: Mercury, Venus, Earth, Mars, Jupiter, Saturn, Uranus, Neptune, and Pluto.

The planets have been divided into two basic groups. There are Earth-like planets and Jupiter-like planets.

Earth-like planets are close to the Sun and are made up of rock and metal. These planets are Mercury, Venus, Earth, and Mars. The other planets are larger and farther away from the Sun. These planets are Jupiter, Saturn, Uranus, and Neptune. These four planets haven't got a solid surface. They are made up of gases and liquids.

But that's only eight planets. Pluto, the farthest from the Sun, is neither Earth-like nor Jupiter-like. It is a frozen planet, the only one.

Each planet **rotates** on its **axis**. An axis is like an imaginary pole going through a planet's centre from one end to the other. The planet spins as if a giant hand had given this pole a great twist.

Most planets rotate from west to east. Only Venus, Uranus, and Pluto rotate from east to west. On these three planets the Sun seems to rise in the west and set in the east.

LEARN MORE! READ THESE ARTICLES...
ASTEROIDS (VOLUME 2) • SOLAR SYSTEM (VOLUME 2)
STARS (VOLUME 2)

DID YOU KNOW?
Scientists have found three planets orbiting the star Upsilon Andromedae, a star much like our Sun. Some think this means there could be life on one of the planets.

SEARCH LIGHT

Group the nine planets according to whether they're made of *Gas, Ice,* or *Rock/Metal.*

Jupiter - Saturn - Mars - Venus - Uranus - Pluto - Earth - Mercury - Neptune

Answer: *Gas:* Jupiter, Saturn, Uranus, Neptune
Ice: Pluto
Rock/Metal: Mars, Venus, Earth, Mercury

The Planet Nearest to the Sun

Mercury is the first of the nine planets in our solar system and the closest to the Sun. Because it seems to move so quickly across the night sky, it was named after the wing-footed Roman god. Mercury is visible to the naked eye from Earth, just before dawn and just after sunset.

Mercury is only slightly bigger than Earth's Moon. Its entire surface is airless, though many different gases surround the planet. Mercury is also a place of extreme temperatures. Its hottest temperature is 400°C and its coldest is −175°C.

In 1974 and 1975 the spacecraft Mariner 10 flew as close to Mercury as possible, sending back pictures and other information.

Why would being the closest planet to the Sun make Mercury hard to study? (Hint: Think of two important things the Sun gives us.)

Mariner 10 space probe, which sent valuable pictures of and other data about Mercury.
© Corbis

Scientists found the planet's surface covered with a layer of broken rock called 'regolith'. Mercury also has large ice patches at its north pole.

Some regions of Mercury are filled with heavy **craters**, probably created when the planet ran into other bodies as it was forming. Other regions show gently rolling plains. These may have been smoothed by the flow of volcanic lava. The planet also features long steep cliffs called 'scarps' in some areas.

Mercury takes 88 Earth days to go around the Sun once, which gives it a very short year. But it takes 1,416 hours to complete one **rotation** about its **axis**, so it has a very long day.

Mercury has a sunrise only once in every two of its years. This is because, after one of its very long days, the Sun is in a different place in Mercury's sky. It takes three of Mercury's days (about 176 of our days) for the Sun to rise once again in the morning sky.

LEARN MORE! READ THESE ARTICLES...
PLANETS (VOLUME 2) • PLUTO (VOLUME 2)
SOLAR SYSTEM (VOLUME 2)

DID YOU KNOW?
It's not surprising that Mercury was named after the speedy messenger of the gods. The planet travels at an incredible 48 kilometres per second.

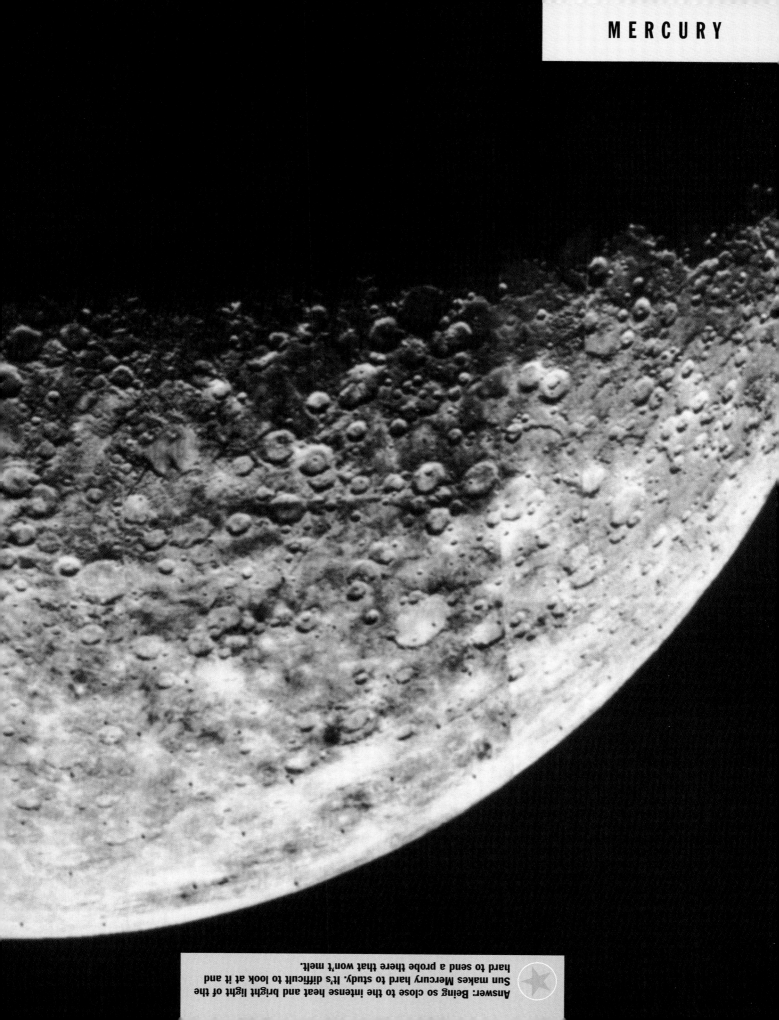

DID YOU KNOW?

Some scientists think that an unusual positioning of the planets Venus and Jupiter may have been the bright Star of Bethlehem reported at the time of Jesus Christ's birth.

A Morning and Evening Star

Venus is the second planet from the Sun. It is named after the Roman goddess of love and beauty, perhaps because it shines so brightly. It shines brightly sometimes in the western sky as the 'evening star' and at other times in the pre-dawn eastern sky as the 'morning star'.

Magellan space probe being launched by the space shuttle *Atlantis* in 1989.
© NASA/Roger Ressmeyer/Corbis

Although Venus is the closest planet to Earth, it is difficult to study because it is completely covered by thick layers of clouds. Venus' dense cloud layers do not allow much sunlight to reach the planet's surface. They do, however, help keep the surface very hot, as do the planet's active volcanoes. The temperature on the Venusian surface reaches about 464°C. The highest clouds, by contrast, have a daily range of 25 to −149°C.

Of all the planets, Venus is closest to Earth in size. In fact, Earth and Venus were once regarded as sister planets. Some scientists have suggested that Venus could support some form of life, perhaps in its clouds. However, people could not breathe the air there.

Several spacecraft have visited and sent back information about Venus, beginning with Mariner 2 in 1962. The immensely powerful Hubble Space Telescope has also provided considerable **data** about the planet.

Scientists have learned that the surface of Venus is marked with hundreds of large meteor **craters**. These craters suggest that since it formed, the surface of Venus has changed in a different way from Earth's surface. Earth has only a few large craters that are easy to recognize.

Venus is different from Earth in another way too. It hasn't got a moon.

SEARCH LIGHT

How are Venus and Earth alike? What makes them different?

LEARN MORE! READ THESE ARTICLES…
MARS (VOLUME 2) • PLANETS (VOLUME 2) • SOLAR SYSTEM (VOLUME 2)

NASA/JPL/Caltech

DID YOU KNOW?
The reason Mars appears red is that the planet's soil contains a lot of rusted iron.

The Red Planet

Mars is the fourth planet from the Sun. It is named after the ancient Roman god of war. Since the planet is red in colour, it is also called the 'red planet'.

The first spacecraft to fly close to Mars was Mariner 4, in 1965. In the 1970s two Viking spacecraft landed there, and in July 1997 Mars Pathfinder touched down. These efforts sent back soil sample reports, pictures, and other **data** from Mars - but no proof of life.

Because of similarities between Mars and Earth, however, scientists think there could be some form of life on Mars.

Mars is half the size of Earth. Its thin air is made up mainly of carbon dioxide and other gases, so we wouldn't be able to breathe it. And the Martian surface is much colder than Earth's would be at that distance from the Sun. Two small moons, Phobos and Deimos, **orbit** Mars.

SEARCH LIGHT

Which surface feature on Mars holds a record?

Martian surface of rocks and fine-grained material, photographed in 1976 by the Viking 1 spacecraft.
NASA

Like Earth, Mars has ice caps at both poles. But its ice caps are composed mostly of solid carbon dioxide, or dry ice. Liquid water has not been seen on the surface of Mars. However, billions of years ago there may have been large lakes or even oceans on Mars.

Also like Earth, Mars has different seasons. Mars takes 687 Earth days to go around the Sun once. This means that its year is almost twice as long as ours. But since it spins on its **axis** once every 24 hours and 37 minutes, its day is just about the same length.

Despite being small, Mars has the largest volcano in our solar system, Olympus Mons. It stands about three times higher than Earth's highest point, Mount Everest, and covers an area just a bit smaller than the entire country of Poland.

LEARN MORE! READ THESE ARTICLES...
EXTRATERRESTRIAL LIFE (VOLUME 2) • SOLAR SYSTEM (VOLUME 2)
SPACECRAFT (VOLUME 2)

In this image taken by the Hubble Space Telescope in 1997, you can see the north polar ice cap (white area) at the top and some huge volcanoes (the darker red spots) in the left half of the photo.
Phil James (Univ. Toledo), Todd Clancy (Space Science Inst., Boulder, CO), Steve Lee (Univ. Colorado), and NASA

Answer: Mars has the largest volcano in our solar system.

King of the Planets

Jupiter is the biggest planet in our solar system. It is so big that all the other eight planets could fit inside it at the same time and there would still be some space left. The planet is named after the king of the Roman gods.

Jupiter is a giant ball of gases, mostly the **elements** hydrogen and helium. Helium is the gas that makes balloons float in air, and hydrogen is

Jupiter's Great Red Spot (colours improved) as seen by Voyager I spacecraft, 1979.
© Jet Propulsion Laboratory/NASA

one part of water. The centre of the planet is probably made of a hot liquid, like a thick soup.

Jupiter isn't a very welcoming place. It is extremely hot. It is thousands of times hotter than the hottest place on Earth.

Also, storms rage on Jupiter's surface almost all the time. Scientists have seen one storm there that is almost twice as wide as the Earth! It is called the Great Red Spot. It has been raging on Jupiter's surface for at least a few hundred years.

Jupiter definitely has over 50 moons, and probably more. Some of them are much bigger than Earth's Moon. One is even bigger than the planet Mercury! Others are tiny, only a few miles across.

Astronomers have found something very exciting on one of Jupiter's moons, called Europa. They believe that it has a huge ocean of water below its surface that may have simple life forms in it.

LEARN MORE! READ THESE ARTICLES…
GALILEO (VOLUME 4) • SATURN (VOLUME 2)
SOLAR SYSTEM (VOLUME 2)

SEARCH LIGHT

Find and correct the mistake in this sentence: A storm known as the Big Red Dog has been raging on Jupiter's surface for hundreds of years.

DID YOU KNOW?
Jupiter has more than 50 known moons and Earth has only 1. But that seems fair because Jupiter is 1,500 times bigger than Earth!

Answer: A storm known as the Great Red Spot has been raging
on Jupiter's surface for hundreds of years.

The Ringed Planet

Saturn is the sixth planet from the Sun. It is named after the god of **agriculture** in Roman mythology. Saturn is easily visible through a small telescope, and its famous spectacular rings are quite clear. The astronomer Galileo was the first to see the rings through his telescope.

Saturn is a gas planet, like Jupiter, Neptune, and Uranus. Very little of it is solid. Most of Saturn consists of the **elements** hydrogen and helium. It is covered with bands of coloured clouds and surrounded by a number of thin rings made up of water ice and ice-covered **particles**. Photographs taken by the Voyager 1 and 2 spacecraft show that these rings range in size from a speck of dust to the size of a house. Voyager 2 took the photograph you see here.

Because Saturn is made of different substances, different parts of the planet **rotate** at different rates. The upper atmosphere swirls around the planet at rates of between 10 hours and 10 minutes (Earth time) and about 10 hours and 40 minutes. The inner core, which is probably made of hot rocks, rotates in about 10 hours and 39 minutes.

Saturn takes 29 years and 5 months in Earth time to go around the Sun just once. The Earth goes around the Sun once every 365 days. Saturn's year is so much longer because the planet is so much farther away from the Sun than Earth is.

Astronomers have found that at least 30 moons **orbit** Saturn. The largest of these is Titan, which is almost as large as the planet Mercury or Mars. In our photograph, you can see two of the moons as tiny white spots to the lower left of (Dione) and below (Rhea) the planet. Other satellites include Mimas, Enceladus, and Tethys.

SEARCH LIGHT

Saturn's many rings are made of
a) ice.
b) dust.
c) gas.
d) rock.

DID YOU KNOW?
Saturn is more than ten times the size of Earth. But the planet is so light that it could float on an ocean of water.

LEARN MORE! READ THESE ARTICLES...
GALILEO (VOLUME 4) • JUPITER (VOLUME 2)
SOLAR SYSTEM (VOLUME 2)

Answer: a) ice.

King George's Star

Uranus is the seventh planet from the Sun. It's named after the god of the heavens in ancient Greek mythology.

When William Herschel discovered this planet in March 1781, he named it Georgium Sidus (George's Star) in honour of King George III of England. Others called it Herschel. In about 1850, scientists began to use the name Uranus.

The spacecraft Voyager 2 visited Uranus about 200 years after Herschel discovered it. Findings confirmed that Uranus is a large gas planet. Small amounts of methane gas in its upper atmosphere give the planet a blue-green colour.

It takes Uranus 84 of Earth's years to go once around the Sun, so its year is 84 times as long as ours. But the planet takes only about 17 hours to spin on its **axis** once, so its day is shorter.

Unlike other planets, Uranus lies on its side at an odd angle. It points first one pole towards the Sun, then its equator, and then the other pole. So it is not yet clear which is the planet's 'north' pole.

Find and correct the mistake in the following sentence: When William Herschel discovered Uranus in 1781, he named it Georgium Sidus after his dog.

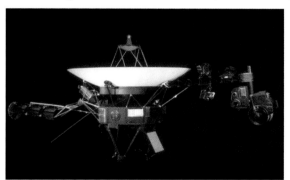

Voyager 2, the spacecraft that reported Uranus' makeup.
© Corbis

As with other gas planets, such as Jupiter, Saturn, and Neptune, Uranus has a system of rings. In some places, the rings are so thin that they seem to disappear.

The planet has 20 known moons that are made mostly of ice and have many **craters**. The five major ones are Miranda, Ariel, Umbriel, Titania, and Oberon. Their names are those of characters from works by William Shakespeare and Alexander Pope.

LEARN MORE! READ THESE ARTICLES…
PLANETS (VOLUME 2) • SATURN (VOLUME 2) • SOLAR SYSTEM (VOLUME 2)

DID YOU KNOW?
Between Uranus and Saturn lies Chiron, an object first considered to be an asteroid, then reclassified as a comet. Its name reflects its confused identity: Chiron was a centaur - a half man, half horse in Greek mythology.

Answer: When William Herschel discovered Uranus in 1781, he named it Georgium Sidus after his king.

The Eighth Planet

Neptune is the eighth planet from the Sun. It is named after the Roman god of the sea.

The planet Neptune was discovered in 1846, but little was known about it until the spacecraft Voyager 2 visited it in August 1989.

Artist's impression of the Voyager 2 spacecraft leaving Neptune after it visited that planet (seen in the background).
© Corbis

Neptune is made up mostly of gases. Its bluish colour comes from its thick atmosphere of hydrogen, helium, and methane. Like other gas planets, such as Jupiter and Saturn, Neptune has rapid winds and big storms. The winds on Neptune are the fastest known in our solar system, reaching speeds of about 2,400 kilometres per hour.

The planet rotates quickly - once every 16.1 hours. This means that its day is about two-thirds as long as ours. But it has a much longer year. There are about 60,225 days in one Neptune year. That's how many days it takes the planet to **orbit** the Sun. It has been in the same year since its discovery in 1846. Each season on Neptune lasts for 41 years.

Like Saturn, Neptune has rings - but they aren't as noticeable. Neptune also has 11 known moons. Triton is the largest moon. Triton is slowly drawing closer to Neptune. It is thought that it will one day crash into the planet.

LEARN MORE! READ THESE ARTICLES...
PLANETS (VOLUME 2) • SATURN (VOLUME 2)
SOLAR SYSTEM (VOLUME 2)

DID YOU KNOW?

It's more than just a little chilly on Neptune. The average temperature is −225°C. By comparison, Antarctica - the coldest place on Earth - has recorded a mere −90°C at its coldest.

SEARCH LIGHT

Neptune has a shorter day than Earth. So why is Neptune's year so much longer than ours? (Hint: Neptune is the eighth planet from the Sun, and Earth is only the third.)

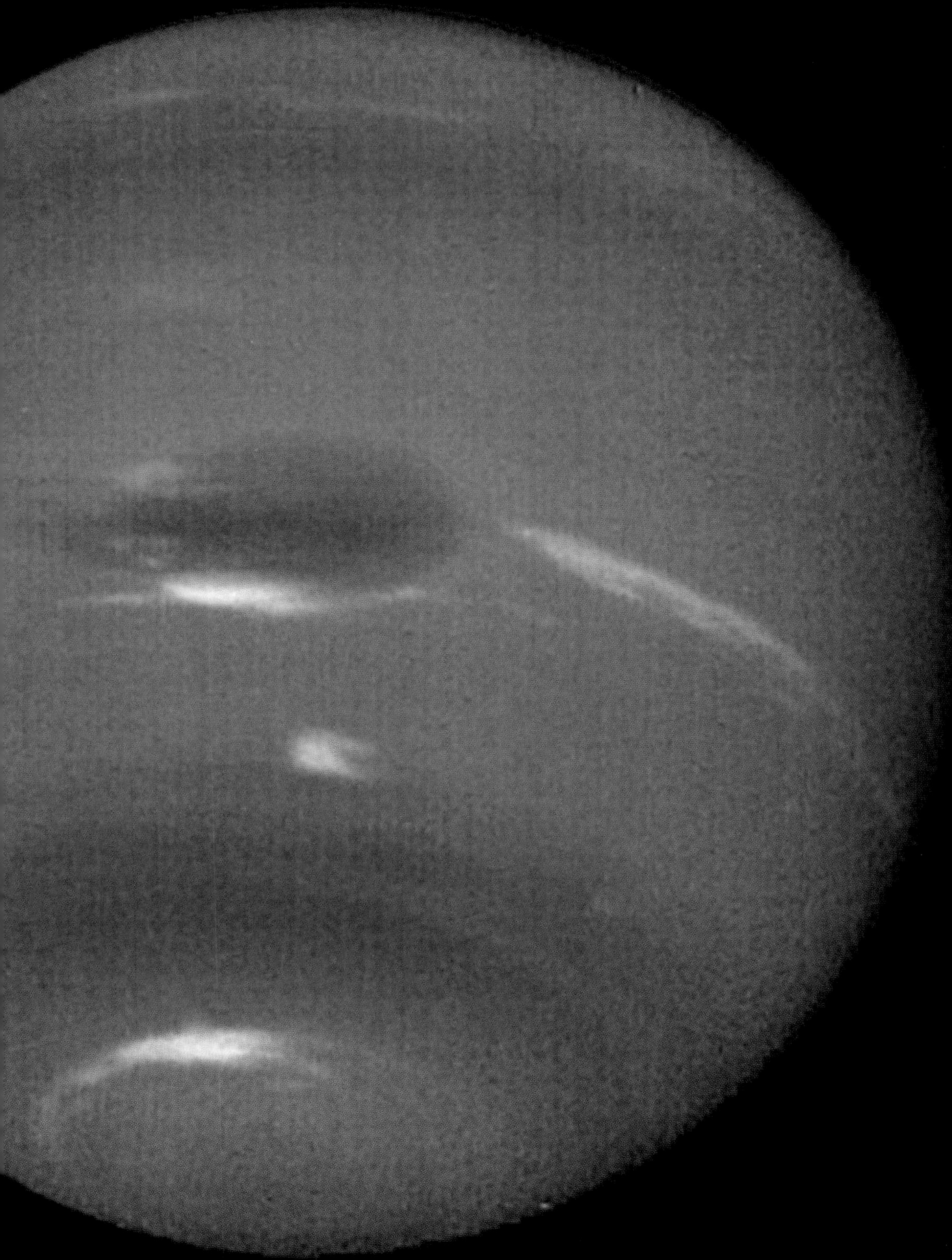

Answer: Neptune is so much farther than Earth from the Sun that it takes the eighth planet about 165 times as long to orbit the Sun.

SEARCH LIGHT

Fill in
the gaps:
Pluto is so
_____
that it wasn't
discovered until
_____.

The Lonely Planet

In Roman mythology, Pluto was the god of the underworld. Pluto is the name given to another dark mystery: the smallest planet in our solar system. Pluto is smaller than the Earth's Moon and is the farthest planet from the Sun - most of the time.

One of the very first photos of Pluto's surface, taken with the Hubble Space Telescope.
Alan Stern (Southwestern Research Institute), Marc Bule (Lowell Observatory), NASA, and the European Space Agency

Every 248 years, Pluto's odd **orbit** takes it closer to the Sun than the planet Neptune goes. For 20 years Neptune becomes the farthest planet, as happened from 1979 to 1999.

Pluto is so far away and small that it wasn't discovered until 1930. It is the only planet that hasn't been visited by a spacecraft. Only recently have very strong instruments like the Hubble Space Telescope given us some details about this mysterious faraway planet.

Tiny Pluto is only about 2,390 kilometres across from pole to pole. It's not entirely clear what the planet is made of, but scientists think it may be 50 to 75 per cent rock and the rest frozen water and gases. Pluto is so far from the Sun's warmth that all of it is permanently frozen. Because of its small size and icy makeup and because it travels in a part of the solar system where some comets are thought to come from, scientists wonder if Pluto is really more like a giant comet than a planet.

Pluto spins in the opposite direction from most of the other planets. If you were on the planet, you would see the Sun rise in the west and set in the east. A day on Pluto is equal to six days and 25 minutes on Earth. Pluto's year takes more than 90,155 of our days.

Pluto's moon, Charon, wasn't discovered until 1978. As you can see from the large photo, Charon is about half the size of Pluto - quite large for a moon. In fact, some scientists consider Pluto and Charon to be a double planet.

DID YOU KNOW?
Walt Disney's dog character Pluto was named after the ninth planet. Pluto the dog first appeared in 1930, the same year that the planet Pluto was discovered.

LEARN MORE! READ THESE ARTICLES...
NEPTUNE (VOLUME 2) • SOLAR SYSTEM (VOLUME 2) • TELESCOPES (VOLUME 2)

Answer: Pluto is so far away that it wasn't discovered until 1930.

Building Blocks
of Matter

Everything in the world is made up of molecules. Our bodies, our clothes, our houses, animals, plants, air, water, sky - everything. Molecules are so small, though, that we can't see them with our naked eyes.

But molecules aren't the smallest things. Molecules are made up of atoms, which are even smaller. Atoms are so small that it would take more than a billion atoms to fill the space taken up by one pea!

The word 'atom' comes from the Greek word *atomos,* meaning '**indivisible**'. But despite what their name suggests, atoms can indeed be divided into smaller pieces. Each atom has a **core**, called a 'nucleus'. Around the nucleus swarm tiny **particles** called 'electrons'. The nucleus itself is made up of other small particles called 'protons' and 'neutrons'. And these protons and neutrons are made up of even smaller things called 'quarks'. So, for now at least, quarks are among the smallest known things in the universe.

LEARN MORE! READ THESE ARTICLES...
MARIE CURIE (VOLUME 4) • ENERGY (VOLUME 2)
NUCLEAR ENERGY (VOLUME 2)

DID YOU KNOW?
Quarks are so small that scientists have to make up new ways to describe them. They talk about the different 'flavours' of quarks - not chocolate or pistachio but 'up', 'down', 'charm', 'strange', 'top' and 'bottom'.

SEARCH LIGHT

True
or false?
Atoms are the
smallest things
of all.

Answer: FALSE. Atoms can be split into electrons, neutrons, and
protons, all of which are smaller than an atom itself. And quarks
are even smaller still.

The Power of Life

Without energy in our bodies, we wouldn't be able to do anything. We couldn't walk, talk, or even play. Energy is usable power. And all energy is related to some kind of motion.

All living things need energy, no matter what they do. Plants get their energy from sunlight. The energy is stored in **chemicals** inside the plant. This happens in a process called 'photosynthesis'.

Animals that eat plants take in the energy stored in plants. The energy is then stored in chemicals inside the animals as 'food energy'. The same happens when animals eat other animals.

Plants and animals use food energy every day as they grow and do the work of being a plant or an animal. So plants have to keep **absorbing** sunlight, and animals have to keep eating plants or other animals.

It isn't only living things that have energy. A dead tree has hidden energy. When we burn its wood it gives off warmth, or 'heat energy'. The Sun also makes heat energy as it constantly burns.

The Sun gives off not just heat but also light, as 'light energy'. The battery in a torch makes it shine, **generating** light energy. But if we put the same battery in a radio, we get music. A battery's energy is known as 'electrical energy'. And in a toy car that electrical energy produces movement, or 'kinetic energy'.

If we couldn't use heat, light, or electrical energy, we wouldn't be able to drive cars or cook food. We wouldn't have light at night. Basically, we'd have to use the energy of our own bodies. And that would mean eating a lot more and doing a lot less.

SEARCH LIGHT

These sentences are mixed up. See if you can sort them out.
Heat energy comes from things people or animals eat.
Food energy comes from things that burn.

LEARN MORE! READ THESE ARTICLES...
LIQUIDS, SOLIDS, AND GASES (VOLUME 2)
STARS (VOLUME 2)
THERMAL POWER (VOLUME 2)

DID YOU KNOW?
Energy from food is measured in calories. An adult needs to take in about 2,000 to 2,500 calories a day. Bicyclists in a major race eat three to five times that much, and still sometimes run out of energy.

Answer: Heat energy comes from things that burn. Food energy comes from things people or animals eat.

The Invisible Magnet

Raise your arm. Keep it in that position for as long as you can. What happens?

After some time, your arm begins to hurt. Something seems to be pulling it down. Soon you will have to lower your arm.

A force called 'gravity' causes you to lower your arm. Gravity acts a bit like a magnet, tugging at your arm as if it were a piece of metal.

We can't see gravity or touch it. We can only feel it. The Earth has gravity that pulls down on everything on or near it. It is this force that keeps us all on the Earth.

The Moon and the Sun also have gravity. All bodies in the universe have gravity. In fact, gravity helps hold all of them together. Sir Isaac Newton first introduced the idea of gravity, and Albert Einstein added to Newton's ideas.

Gravity works in a two-way system. This means that all bodies exert a pull on each other. For example, Earth's gravity forces the Moon to circle around it all the time. In return, the Moon's gravity attracts the waters of Earth's oceans to cause tides.

The force of gravity becomes weaker and weaker as you move away from its source. That is partly why astronauts can float around in outer space. They are too far away for the Earth to have much pull on them.

What do you think would happen if there were no gravity on Earth?

LEARN MORE! READ THESE ARTICLES...
ALBERT EINSTEIN (VOLUME 4)
SIR ISAAC NEWTON (VOLUME 4) • TIDES (VOLUME 1)

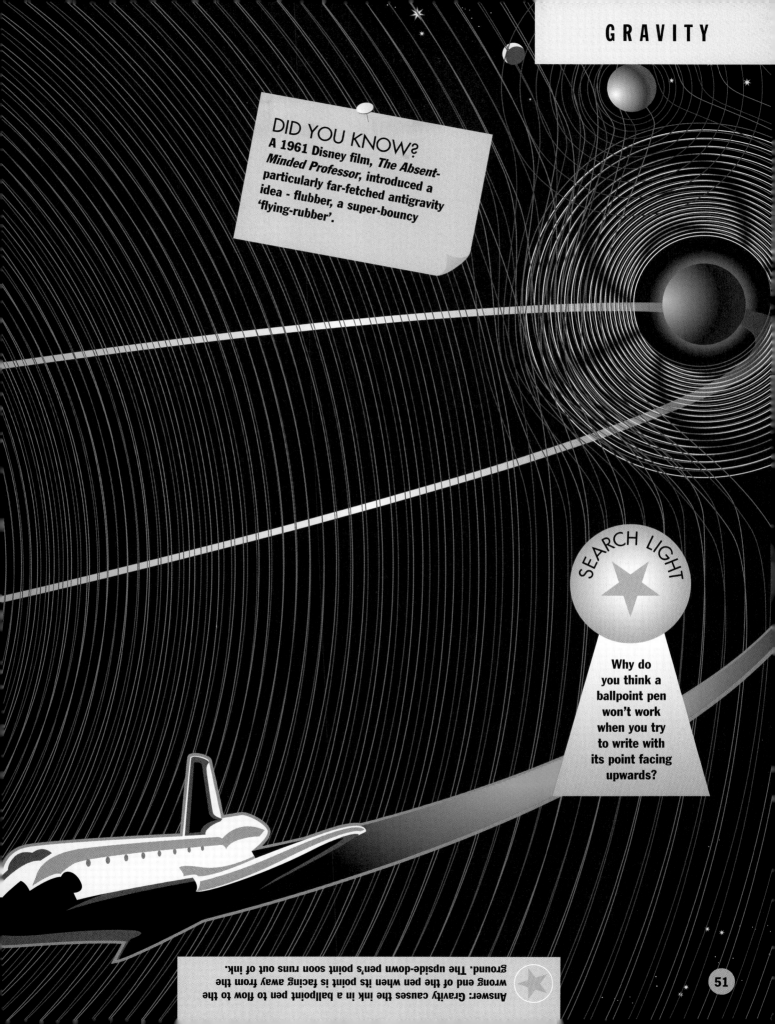

DID YOU KNOW?
A 1961 Disney film, *The Absent-Minded Professor*, introduced a particularly far-fetched antigravity idea - flubber, a super-bouncy 'flying-rubber'.

SEARCH LIGHT

Why do you think a ballpoint pen won't work when you try to write with its point facing upwards?

Answer: Gravity causes the ink in a ballpoint pen to flow to the wrong end of the pen when its point is facing away from the ground. The upside-down pen's point soon runs out of ink.

Same Stuff, Different Forms

Did you know that many of the things you may see or use every day - such as the water in a glass, the air in a football, and even the hard metal in a toy car - are **potential** transformers?

The substances that these things are made of can take the form of a solid, a liquid, or a gas. The form they take depends mostly on their temperature. When water gets cold enough, it becomes a hard solid we call 'ice'. When it gets hot enough, it becomes a wispy gas we call 'steam'. Many other substances behave the same way when they are heated or cooled enough.

A solid holds its own size and shape without needing a container. If you pour water into an ice tray and freeze it, the water will keep the shape of the cube-shaped moulds in the tray. You can think of the solid metal in a toy car as frozen too, but its melting temperature is much higher than the temperatures we live in. The person who made the car poured very hot liquid metal into a car-shaped mould and let it cool down and freeze.

A liquid does not hold its own shape. If you pour a half litre of water into a tall vase or a shallow bowl, it will take the shape of its container. But that water does keep its own size. It measures a half litre. Everyday liquids such as milk, paint, and petrol act this same way.

Gases do not keep their own shape or their own size. When air is pumped into a football, it takes the shape and size of the ball. As more air is pumped in, the ball gets harder but not much bigger. The air changes its size to fit the space inside the ball.

LEARN MORE!
READ THESE ARTICLES...
TEMPERATURES (VOLUME 2)
THERMAL POWER (VOLUME 2)
VOLCANOES (VOLUME 1)

SEARCH LIGHT

Write down whether each item in the list describes a solid (S), a liquid (L), or a gas (G). Some may match more than one state.

- melts
- freezes
- has its own shape
- pours
- floats in air
- spreads out
- has an odour

DID YOU KNOW?

If you've ever smelled gas coming from a cooker, you know it has an odd odour. But cooking gas has no odour. What you're smelling is another gas with an odour that's easy to notice. It's mixed with the cooking gas so that people know when there's a leak.

Answer: melts = S; freezes = L; has its own shape = S; floats in air = G; pours = L; spreads out = L, G; has an odour = G

Temperature measures how much
a) heat something has.
b) chill something has.
c) pressure something has.

DID YOU KNOW?

If you test too-hot bath water with your foot, you're likely to burn that foot. That's because it takes longer for your foot to recognize temperature than it does your hand.

Hot and Cold

We can use our fingers, our tongue, or almost any part of our skin to feel just how hot or how cold something is. This is important because our bodies need just the right amount of heat so that we can live comfortably.

When it's cold and we want to make a room warmer, we turn on the heater. In the summer when it's hot and we want to make the room cooler, do we add cold to the room?

No. We take away some of the heat. We say something is cold when it doesn't have much heat. The less heat it has, the colder it is.

Air conditioners suck hot air from a room. Pipes inside the air conditioners take a lot of heat out of the air, making it cold. Then a blower fans the cooled air into the room again.

When we want to know exactly how hot or how cold something is, we use a thermometer. A thermometer tells us about temperature - that is, how hot something is. Some countries measure temperature in 'degrees Celsius (°C)'. Others use a different measuring system of 'degrees Fahrenheit (°F)'.

We can use thermometers to measure air temperature, oven temperature, even body temperature. And your body temperature tells not only whether you feel hot or cold but whether you're healthy.

LEARN MORE! READ THESE ARTICLES...
LIQUIDS, SOLIDS, AND GASES (VOLUME 2)
MEASUREMENT (VOLUME 2) • THERMAL POWER (VOLUME 2)

Cables, Fuses, Wires, and Energy

You can't see electricity, but you know it's there when you watch an electric light go on, hear the telephone ring, or watch the television.

Electricity comes into your house through thick wires called 'cables'. These join a **fuse** box. From the fuse box run all the electric wires for your house. Each wire connects to a plug socket or a switch. From there, electricity passes along the plugs and leads that go into an appliance, lamp, or television.

Electricity moves easily along things made of metal, such as silver, copper, or iron. That's why copper wires are used to carry the electricity. Electricity doesn't pass through rubber or plastic. That's why wires carrying electricity are usually coated with rubber or plastic.

This coating is important, because electricity will flow wherever it can. When it is loose, it can be very dangerous. It can cause shocks, start fires, or even kill.

Did you know that electricity can be used to make a magnet? If a wire is wound into a coil and wrapped around a piece of iron, the iron will become a magnet when electricity is sent through the coil. The iron will then attract other things made of iron and steel. Such a magnet is called an 'electromagnet'.

As soon as the electricity is turned off, the electromagnet isn't a magnet anymore. If the magnet is holding something when the electricity is turned off, that thing will drop.

SEARCH LIGHT

Fill in the gaps: To prevent shocks, electric wires should be wrapped with _____ or _____.

LEARN MORE! READ THESE ARTICLES…
THUNDER AND LIGHTNING (VOLUME 1) • WATER POWER (VOLUME 2)
WIND POWER (VOLUME 2)

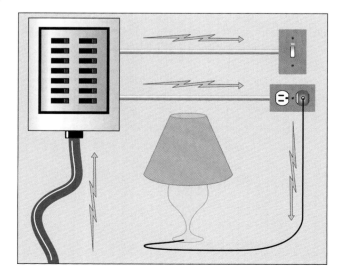

DID YOU KNOW?
Although Thomas Edison is better known for his light bulb, films, and phonograph, his first invention was an electric voting machine.

Answer: To prevent shocks, electric wires should be wrapped with rubber or plastic.

DID YOU KNOW?
A NASA probe to Mars ended up crashing because the two teams of scientists working on it used different measurement systems. One team used metric and the other used the Imperial system, so directions given to the probe sent it too close to the planet.

SEARCH LIGHT

Guess which unit of measure was originally defined as equal to 'an average throwing stone'.
a) a pound
b) a cup
c) an inch

Understanding Size and Distance

How far away from you is the nearest chair? You can make your own measurement to find out how many shoes away the chair is.

Stand up where you are and face the chair. Count 'one' for your right shoe. Now place the heel of your left shoe against the toe of your right shoe and count 'two'. Continue stepping, heel-to-toe, right then left, counting each shoe length, until you get to the chair.

Centuries ago, people did just what you are doing now. They used parts of the body to measure things. An inch was about the width of a man's thumb. A foot was the length of his foot. A yard was the distance from the tip of his nose to the end of his thumb when his arm was stretched out. But since everyone's thumbs, feet, and arms were different sizes, so were everyone's inches, feet, and yards!

Finally, in the 1800s, all these terms were standardised - that is, everyone in England agreed on a specific definition for each one. They became part of the English system of measurement, called the British **Imperial** System.

We also use another system, called the 'metric system'. This measures in centimetres and metres, grams and kilograms, and litres. All these measurements can be multiplied or divided by 10. Fortunately, most of the world accepts the metric system or the Imperial system as the **standard** of measurement. So, we know today that one measurement will mean the same thing, no matter where it is used or who's doing the measuring.

LEARN MORE! READ THESE ARTICLES…
CALENDAR (VOLUME 2) • COMPUTERS (VOLUME 2)
TEMPERATURES (VOLUME 2)

Answer: a) a pound. Though people agreed on a pound as the weight of 'an average throwing stone,' there were actually as many different 'pounds' as there were people!

Looking to Nature for Remedies

Two visitors watched a jaguar fall off its tree limb and lie quietly on the ground. Their guide in this South American forest had brought the cat down with a blowgun dart tipped with curare. Made from certain trees in the jungle, curare **paralyses** the muscles in the body.

When scientists heard about this remarkable poison, they experimented with it. Although large doses of curare are deadly, they found that tiny doses can help people relax during **surgery**.

Many years ago, a doctor might have treated stomach-ache with a medicine containing a pinch of gold dust, a spoonful of ash from a dried lizard, 20 powdered beetles, some burned cat's hair, and two mashed onions!

Not all the old recipes for medicine were as bad as this one. Usually medicines were made from tree bark and leaves, berries and seeds, roots, and flowers. The value of some 'folk remedies' has not been proved scientifically, but many modern drugs have been developed from plants, animals, and **minerals**.

The photograph, for example, shows a common flower called 'foxglove'. Its leaves are used to make 'digitalis', which helps people with heart disease. Pods of the opium poppy are used to make painkillers.

Not so long ago, a very important medicine was discovered in mouldy bread. This medicine, penicillin, and others like it are called 'antibiotics'. They help fight many diseases by killing **bacteria**.

Today, most medicines are synthesized. This means that they are made from combinations of chemicals rather than from plants or animals. This method is much more **economical** and allows scientists to create much larger supplies of important medicines.

SEARCH LIGHT

Find and correct the mistake in the following sentence: Many medicines today still come from the bark of animals.

LEARN MORE! READ THESE ARTICLES...
MARIE CURIE (VOLUME 4) • LOUIS PASTEUR (VOLUME 4)
RAINFORESTS (VOLUME 1)

DID YOU KNOW?
Deadly nightshade is a highly poisonous plant that was often used in small amounts as a medicine. It is closely related to the tomato.

Big Energy
from a Small Source

All **matter** is made up of tiny particles called 'molecules'. In turn, all molecules are made up of even tinier particles called 'atoms'.

The central part of an atom is called a 'nucleus'. When the nucleus splits in two, it produces enormous energy. This breaking apart is called 'nuclear fission'. If two nuclei join and form a bigger nucleus - in a process called 'nuclear fusion' - even more energy is produced.

The nuclear energy released from fission and fusion is called 'radiation'. Radiation - the process of giving off **rays** - is a powerful spreading of heat, light, sound, or even invisible beams.

SEARCH LIGHT

What is the main problem with nuclear energy?

One of the first uses of nuclear energy was to build deadly weapons. Atomic bombs built during World War II and dropped on Hiroshima and Nagasaki in Japan largely destroyed those cities and killed many thousands of people. People worldwide now try to make sure that this will never happen again.

Today, however, nuclear energy has many helpful uses. Nuclear power plants produce low-cost electricity. Nuclear energy also fuels submarines. And it has also allowed doctors to see more details inside the body than ever before.

But nuclear energy has its **drawbacks**. Nuclear energy produces nuclear waste. Living beings exposed to the waste can suffer from radiation poisoning. They may experience damaged blood and organs, effects that can be deadly. And the radiation can remain active for thousands of years wherever nuclear waste is thrown away.

Unfortunately, no country has yet discovered the perfect way to store nuclear waste. But the benefits make it worthwhile to keep trying.

DID YOU KNOW?
We all actually enjoy the benefits of nuclear energy every day. The Sun, like all stars, is simply a giant nuclear power plant. Its heat and light are the products of nuclear energy.

LEARN MORE! READ THESE ARTICLES...
ATOMS (VOLUME 2) • MARIE CURIE (VOLUME 4)
STARS (VOLUME 2)

Nuclear power plant on the coast of California, U.S.
© Galen Rowell/Corbis

Answer: Nuclear energy produces poisonous waste that remains deadly for generations. No one has yet come up with a safe and highly reliable way to get rid of the waste.

Energy from Heat

Energy means power - the power to do work. And thermal, or heat, energy can do a lot of work. When heat is applied to water, for instance, it makes the water boil. Boiling water then changes to vapour, or steam, which can apply great force as it escapes a container. Large quantities of steam powered the earliest train engines.

The most important source of thermal energy for our Earth is the Sun's rays. This 'solar energy' is used to heat houses, water,

Fill in the gap: When steam escapes, it gives a mighty push. This push is so strong that it was used to move the early _____ engines.

and, in some countries, ovens used for cooking. Solar power can even be **converted** to electricity and stored for later use.

(Top) Sun's heat focussed and used for cooking on solar oven by Tibetan monk. (Bottom) Locomotive fireman shovels coal to burn, boiling water to produce steam power.

To people, the second most important source of thermal energy is the store of natural fuels on and in the Earth. When these fuels (mainly coal, oil, gas, and wood) are burned, they produce heat. This heat can be used for warmth, made to power a machine directly, or converted into electricity. For example, a car engine burns petroleum (an oil product) for direct thermal power. In some areas, coal is burned to produce the electricity that powers people's homes.

In a very few parts of the world, an interesting third form of heat energy comes from 'living' heat inside the Earth itself. This 'geothermal energy' comes from such sources as natural hot springs and the heat of active volcanoes ('geo-' means 'earth'). Naturally escaping steam and hot water are used to heat and power homes and businesses in Reykjavik, Iceland. And though volcanoes are mostly too hot to tap directly, worldwide experiments continue as other major fuel supplies **dwindle**.

LEARN MORE! READ THESE ARTICLES...
OIL (VOLUME 2) • REYKJAVIK (VOLUME 6) • VOLCANOES (VOLUME 1)

The intense power of the Earth's heat energy sometimes bursts into geysers - hot springs that send roaring columns of steam and boiling water high above the surface. This geyser is the famous Old Faithful in Yellowstone National Park in Wyoming, U.S.

DID YOU KNOW?

Hot-air ballooning, a popular sport in the 1960s, relies on thermal power. A gas burner heats air that is then fed into a large airtight balloon. And because hot air rises, the balloon rises up and away - carrying people or cargo along in its basket or container.

Answer: When steam escapes, it gives a mighty push. This push is so strong that it was used to move the early train engines.

65

DID YOU KNOW?
Apparently, the earliest mention of a waterwheel comes from Greece in 4000 BC. It was used to grind grain.

Streams of Energy

We have only to hear the roar of a waterfall to guess at the power of water. Its force is also clear anytime we see the damage caused by floods. But the water power can be extremely useful as well as destructive.

One excellent aspect of water power is that the water can be reused. Unlike such fuels as coal and oil, water does not get used up when **harnessed** for power. And it doesn't pollute the air either.

The power of water lies not in the water itself but in the flow of water. The power produced by water depends upon the water's

Fill in the gap: Unlike petrol or coal, water power doesn't cause air _____.

© Hubert Stadler/Corbis

weight and its height of fall, called 'head'. Generally, the faster that water moves, the more power it can generate. That's why water flowing from a higher place to a lower place, as a waterfall does, can produce so much energy.

Since ancient times people have used the energy of water to grind wheat and other grains. They first **devised** the waterwheel, a wheel with paddles around its rim. As the photograph shows, the wheel was mounted on a frame over a river. The flowing water striking the blades turned the wheel.

Later, larger waterwheels were used to run machines in factories. They were not very reliable, however. Floodwaters could create too much power, whereas long rainless periods left the factories without any power at all.

Today, streamlined metal waterwheels called 'turbines' help produce electricity. The electricity produced by water is called 'hydroelectric power' ('hydro-' means 'water'). Enormous dams, like the one pictured here, provide this **superior** source of electricity.

LEARN MORE! READ THESE ARTICLES…
ELECTRICITY (VOLUME 2) • TSUNAMIS (VOLUME 1)
VICTORIA FALLS (VOLUME 8)

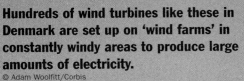

Hundreds of wind turbines like these in Denmark are set up on 'wind farms' in constantly windy areas to produce large amounts of electricity.
© Adam Woolfitt/Corbis

SEARCH LIGHT

Which of the following are advantages of wind power? It's inexpensive. It works everywhere. It's clean. It's endless.

DID YOU KNOW?
The total wind power of our atmosphere, at any one time, is estimated to be 3.6 billion kilowatts. That's enough energy to light 36 billion light bulbs all at once.

Energy in the Air

Wind power has been used for many hundreds of years. Its energy has filled the sails of ships and powered machines that grind grain, pump water, drain marshes, saw wood, and make paper. Wind provides a clean and endless source of energy.

In the 1890s windmills in Denmark became the first to use wind power to generate electricity. But it took the major energy crisis of the 1970s to focus people's thoughts seriously again on using wind energy to produce electricity.

Traditional windmills in the Netherlands.
© ML Sinibaldi/Corbis

Windmills provide power to make electricity when their sails are turned by wind blowing against them. Originally, the sails were long narrow sheets of canvas stretched over a wooden frame. Later windmills used different materials and designs. Usually there are four sails shaped like large blades.

When the sails turn, the axle they are attached to turns as well, much as car wheels turn on their axles. The axle causes various **gears** to turn, which then causes a large crankshaft to turn. The crankshaft is a long pole running the length of the windmill tower. At its other end the crankshaft is attached to a generator, a motor that can make and store electricity. So when the wind blows, the generator runs - making electricity.

Today, modern efficient wind machines called 'wind turbines' are used to generate electricity. These machines have from one to four blades and operate at high speeds. The first of these wind turbines appeared in the mid-1990s.

LEARN MORE! READ THESE ARTICLES...
CYCLONES AND TORNADOES (VOLUME 1) • NETHERLANDS (VOLUME 6) • SHIPS (VOLUME 2)

Answer: Wind power is inexpensive, clean, and endless. Unfortunately, it's not a usable way to generate power in areas with little or no wind.

SEARCH LIGHT

What modern machine's name sounds a lot like 'ornithopter', the flapping-wing machine that people tried to fly?

The First Flights

From the earliest times people wanted to fly, but no one knew how. Some people thought it would help if their arms were more like bird wings. So they strapped large feathery wings to their arms. Not one left the ground. A few even tried machines with flapping wings, called 'ornithopters'. These didn't work either.

Then in 1799 a British scientist named Sir George Cayley wrote a book and drew pictures explaining how birds use their wings and the speed of the wind to fly. About a hundred years later, two American brothers named Orville and Wilbur Wright read Cayley's book. Although they were bicycle makers, they decided to build a flying machine.

The Wright brothers' machine, *Flyer I*, had the strong light wings of a **glider**, a petrol-powered engine, and two **propellers**. Then, from a list of places where strong winds blow, they selected the Kill Devil Hills near Kitty Hawk, North Carolina, U.S., as the site of their experiment.

In 1903 Orville, lying flat on the lower wing of *Flyer I*, flew a distance of 37 metres. That first flight lasted only 12 seconds. The next year the Wrights managed to fly their second 'aeroplane', *Flyer II*, nearly 5 kilometres over a period of 5 minutes and 4 seconds.

Soon Glenn Curtiss, another American bicycle maker, made a faster airplane called the '1909 type'. Not long after that Louis Blériot from France did something no one had tried before. He flew his plane across the English Channel. He was the first man to fly across the sea.

The age of flight had begun.

LEARN MORE! READ THESE ARTICLES…

BIRDS (VOLUME 11) • SHIPS (VOLUME 2) • SPACECRAFT (VOLUME 2)

> **DID YOU KNOW?**
> In 1986 Dick Rutan and Jeana Yeager made the first non-stop round-the-world flight in an airplane. They did the whole trip without refuelling.

The Wright brothers had read that wind was very important for flying. That's why they chose the windy hill in North Carolina, U.S., to test their machines.
© Bettmann/Corbis

Answer: How about the 'helicopter'? The '-opter' part of both words means 'wing'. A helicopter's name means 'whirling wing'. An ornithopter's name means 'bird wing'.

How Henry Ford Made the American Car

Henry Ford was born near Dearborn, Michigan, U.S., in July 1863. As a boy, he loved to play with watches, clocks, and machines - good experience for the person who would build the first affordable car.

Cars had already been built in Europe when Ford experimented with his first **vehicle** in 1899. It had wheels like a bicycle's and a petrol-powered engine that made it move. It was called a Quadricycle and had only two speeds and no reverse.

Within four years Ford had started the Ford Motor Company. His ideas about making cars would change history.

Car makers at the time used parts others had made and put them all together. Ford's company made each and every part that went into their cars. What's more, they made sure that each kind of part was exactly the same.

In 1908 Ford introduced the Model T car. This car worked well and was not costly. It was a big success, but the company couldn't make them quickly enough to satisfy Henry Ford.

In 1913 he started a large factory that made use of his most important idea: the assembly line. Instead of having workers go from car to car, the cars moved slowly down a line while workers stood in place adding parts to them. Each worker added a different part until a whole car was put together.

This meant more cars could be built more quickly at a lower cost. By 1918 half of all cars in the United States were Model Ts. Ford's company had become the largest automobile manufacturer in the world. And Ford had revolutionized the process of **manufacturing**.

SEARCH LIGHT

True or false? Henry Ford built the very first automobile.

LEARN MORE! READ THESE ARTICLES…
AIRPLANES (VOLUME 2) • OIL (VOLUME 2)
TRANSPORTATION (VOLUME 2)

DID YOU KNOW?
Henry Ford is reported to have once said that his customers could get a Model T in 'any colour they like, as long as it's black'.

**Henry Ford's first car was the Quadricycle,
seen here with Ford driving. It had only two
forward speeds and could not back up.**
© Underwood & Underwood/Corbis

Answer: FALSE. Henry Ford built the first inexpensive automobile.
Gottlieb Daimler, a German, gets credit for building the very first
automobile.

SEARCH LIGHT

Louis Braille
invented his
Braille alphabet
when he was 15.
At that age, how
many years had he
been blind?

Books to Touch

More than 175 years ago in France, a young Louis Braille thought of a way to help blind people read and write. He himself could not see. He had hurt his eyes when he was just 3 years old. He was playing with his father's tools, and one of them blinded him forever.

Fortunately, Louis was a clever child. When he was 10 years old, he won a **scholarship** to the National Institute for Blind Children in Paris.

At the school Louis heard about how Captain Barbier, an army officer, had invented a system of writing that used dots. It was called 'night writing', and it helped soldiers read messages in the dark. These messages were of small bump-like dots pressed on a sheet of paper. The dots were easy to make and could be felt quickly.

Louis decided to use similar dots to make an alphabet for the blind. It was slow to be accepted but eventually was a great success. His alphabet used 63 different dot patterns to represent letters, numbers, punctuation, and several other useful signs. People could even learn to read music by feeling dots.

Today blind people all over the world can learn the Braille alphabet. Look at these dots:

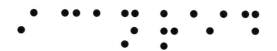

In an actual Braille book, the tips of your fingers would be able to cover each small group of dots.

Can you guess what this pattern of dot letters spells?

It spells the words 'I can read'.

DID YOU KNOW?
On their Web site, the American Foundation for the Blind has a great area where you can learn Braille yourself. Go to http://afb.org and click on 'Braille Bug'.

Answer: Louis Braille had been blind for 12 years when he invented his alphabet.

75

SEARCH LIGHT

What was probably the earliest use for calendars?

Charting the Year

A calendar, like a clock, provides a way to count time - though calendars count days and months rather than minutes and hours. The modern calendar has 12 months of 30 or 31 days each (February has 28, sometimes 29). The calendar year has 365 days, which is about how long it takes the Earth to circle the Sun once. That makes it a **solar** calendar.

DID YOU KNOW?
The Chinese calendar names each year for one of 12 animals. In order, these are: rat, ox, tiger, hare, dragon, snake, horse, sheep, monkey, fowl, dog, and pig. The year 2003 is the Year of the Sheep (or Ram), 2004 the Year of the Monkey, and so on.

Today's calendar, with a few changes, has been in use since 1582. Pope Gregory XIII had it designed to correct errors in the previous calendar. For this reason it is called the 'Gregorian calendar'.

The oldest calendars were used to work out when to plant, harvest, and store crops. These were often '**lunar** calendars', based on the number of days it took the Moon to appear full and then **dwindle** away again.

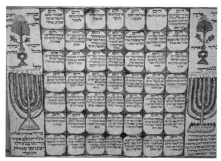

Jewish calendar (in Hebrew) from the 1800s.
© Archivo Iconografico, S.A./Corbis

The traditional Chinese calendar is a lunar calendar. It has 354 days, with months of either 29 or 30 days.

Many calendars have religious origins. In Central and South America, the ancient Aztec and Mayan calendars marked **ritual** days and celebrations. Jews, Muslims, and Hindus have religious calendars - each with a different number of days and months.

All these calendars have one thing in common: they're wrong. None of them measures the Earth's yearlong journey around the Sun precisely. Extra days must be added to keep the count in step with the actual seasons. We add an extra day to February every four years. (Actually, even our corrections are wrong. Once every 400 years we *don't* add that day.)

But if we didn't make some kind of correction, we'd eventually have New Year's Eve in the middle of the year!

LEARN MORE! READ THESE ARTICLES...
MAYAN CIVILIZATION (VOLUME 4) • MEASUREMENT (VOLUME 2) • MOON (VOLUME 2)

This ancient Aztec calendar stone weighs about 25 tons. Its central image of the Aztec sun god, Tonatiuh, indicates the important role religion plays in how major civilizations measure time.
© Randy Faris/Corbis

Answer: The earliest calendars were likely used to tell the right time to plant and harvest crops.

SEARCH LIGHT

Find and
correct the
mistake in the
following sentence:
A set of instructions
that a computer uses
to solve problems
and do work is called
'memory'.

The Machines That Solve Problems

The first computers were expensive room-sized machines that only business and government offices could afford. Today most computers are smaller, and many people have one in their own home or school. These 'personal computers' (PCs) first appeared in the mid-1970s.

A Palm Pilot, one of the tiny but powerful modern computers.
© RNT Productions/Corbis

Computers can find the answers to many maths problems and can simplify work that has many steps and would otherwise take lots of time. They can do this because they can remember, in order, the individual steps of even long and complicated instructions.

The sets of instructions for computers are called 'programs' or 'software'. A computer's brain is its microprocessor - a tiny electronic **device** that reads and carries out the program's instructions.

Because they are programmed in advance, you can use computers to solve maths problems, remember facts, and play games. Computers can also help you draw, write essays, and make your own greeting cards.

Computers need two kinds of memory. 'Main memory' is what handles the information that the computer is using as it is doing its work. Main memory operates amazingly fast and powerfully to speed up a computer's work. The second kind of computer memory is **storage** for its programs and for the results of its operations. The most important storage space is on the computer's hard drive, or hard disk. CD-ROMs and floppy disks are removable storage devices.

Since 1990 very small computers have been developed. Today there are laptop or notebook computers, as well as handheld computers. Handheld computers weigh only a few grams, but they can handle more **data** more quickly that most of the first giant computers.

DID YOU KNOW?
It was a weaving machine, a loom, that led to the first computers. At one time, looms used punched cards to set weaving patterns. Early computers used this system of coding in their 'programming languages'.

LEARN MORE! READ THESE ARTICLES...
ELECTRICITY (VOLUME 2) • INTERNET (VOLUME 2)
PRINTING (VOLUME 2)

Answer: A set of instructions that a computer uses to solve problems and do work is called a 'program' [or 'software'].

Network of People

You can do things with your friends and family even when they are thousands of kilometres away simply by sitting at your computer. The Internet makes this possible.

As the name suggests, the Internet is like a large net whose every strand connects to a different computer. It is an international web linking millions of computer users around the world. Together with the World Wide Web (WWW, or Web), it is used for sending and receiving e-mail and for sharing information on almost any topic.

The Web is an enormous electronic library from which anyone connected to the Internet can receive information. It is organised into tens of millions of sites, each identified by an electronic address called the 'uniform resource locator' (URL). The Web allows you to view photographs and films, listen to songs and hear people speak, and find out about **countless** different things you never knew before.

The Internet has come a long way since 1969, when it all began. At that time the U.S. Defense Department was testing **methods** of making their computers survive a military attack. Soon their networks were extended to various research computers around the United States and then to countries around the world.

By early 1990 the Internet and the World Wide Web had entered homes. Today many people wonder how they ever managed without the Internet.

LEARN MORE! READ THESE ARTICLES...
COMPUTERS (VOLUME 2)
RADIO (VOLUME 2)
TELEPHONES (VOLUME 2)

DID YOU KNOW?
Radio took about 38 years to gain 50 million listeners. TV took about 13 years to have 50 million viewers. The Internet took only 4 years to get 50 million users.

SEARCH LIGHT

The Internet
is more than
a) 10 years old.
b) 20 years old.
c) 30 years old.

Photos That Move

Sitting in a darkened cinema, caught up in the adventures of Harry Potter and Hermione Granger, you might find it difficult to believe that you're watching a series of still photographs. These still photos are projected onto the screen so fast, one after another, that you're tricked into seeing movement. This is why early on they were called 'motion pictures' or 'movies'.

Film for shooting cinema comes in long wound **spools** or **cartridges**. The film takes pictures at either 18 or 24 shots per second. Sometimes there are three or four cameras that shoot a scene from different angles. Sound is recorded at the same time but with separate equipment.

Later, the film is **edited** by cutting out parts that the director doesn't want. The parts being kept are then put together to tell the story. The

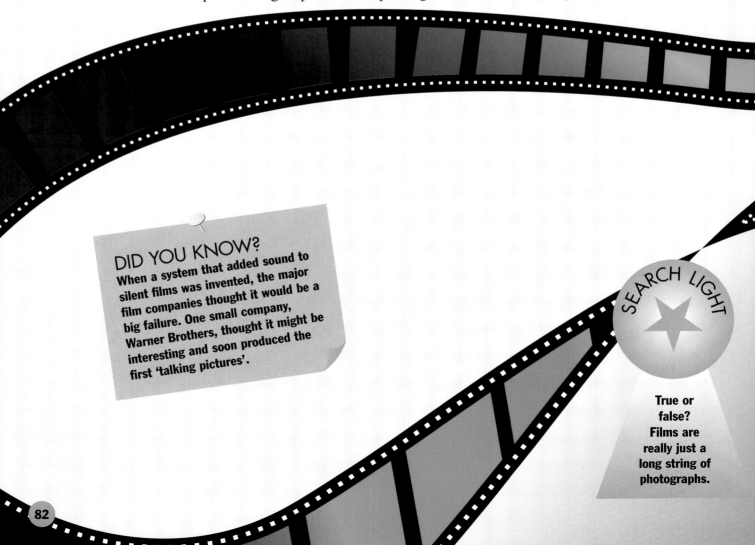

DID YOU KNOW?
When a system that added sound to silent films was invented, the major film companies thought it would be a big failure. One small company, Warner Brothers, thought it might be interesting and soon produced the first 'talking pictures'.

SEARCH LIGHT

True or false? Films are really just a long string of photographs.

finished film, with the sound and the pictures joined together, is shown as a continuous piece.

Film-making is a long and complicated process, involving many people. The actors are the most visible, but there are many others as well. The director has total control over how the story is filmed. A whole crew of people help with costumes, choreography, lighting, sound, camera operations, special effects, and the actors' makeup and hairstyles.

After the film has been shot, there are different people to edit it and other people who advertise the movie. Finally, the film reaches the cinemas. There you buy your popcorn or other refreshments and settle into your seat to enjoy the magic world of the finished film.

LEARN MORE! READ THESE ARTICLES...
CINEMA (VOLUME 3) • PHOTOGRAPHY (VOLUME 2) • TELEVISION (VOLUME 2)

Answer: TRUE. When the string of photos is flashed by quickly, the pictures appear to move.

From the Ground
to the Petrol Station

Up comes the thick black oil from the oil well and...out pours the petrol into your family's car. But how does the oil become fuel for vehicles?

Petroleum, or crude oil, is oil as it is found deep within the Earth. This raw form has many unwanted substances in it that must eventually be removed in a process called 'refining'.

From wells drilled deep into the ground, the oil often goes through long underground pipelines. There are pipelines in some very surprising places - under streets, mountains, deserts, frozen lands, and even lakes and rivers.

Pumping stations keep the thick oil moving through the pipes. Each station gives the oil enough of a push for it to reach the next station. There are pumping stations built all along the pipelines. Here and there along the pipelines, oil is directed into smaller pipes that take it to huge storage tanks.

From the storage tanks, the oil goes to a **refinery**, where it is heated until it is very hot. The hot oil is separated into many different substances. The heavy part that settles down at the bottom is used for road building. Other parts become machine oils and waxes. **Paraffin** and petrol also separate as the oil is heated. Finally, the lightest parts of the oil - cooking gas and other types of gas - are collected.

From the refineries, more pipelines carry oil to round storage tanks in tank farms. Petrol tankers fill up at the storage tanks and take the fuel to petrol stations, where people can fill the tanks in their cars.

LEARN MORE! READ THESE ARTICLES...
AUTOMOBILES (VOLUME 2) • GEOLOGY (VOLUME 1) • POLLUTION (VOLUME 1)

SEARCH LIGHT

Put the different stages in the correct order, beginning with the oil well. (Start) oil well → *pipelines, petrol station, pipelines, refinery, storage tank, pumping station*

Answer: oil well ← pipelines ← pumping station ← storage tank ← refinery ← pipelines ← petrol station

Turning Trees to Paper

The pages in your exercise book are made of paper that came from a factory. So are the pages of this book.

The factory got the paper from a paper mill. The mill probably made the paper from logs. And the logs were cut from trees that grew in a forest. Pine trees are often used to make paper.

If you visit a **traditional** paper mill, you will see people working at large noisy machines that peel bark off the logs and then cut the wood into smaller pieces. Other machines press and grind this wood into very tiny pieces that can be mashed together like potatoes. This gooey stuff is called 'wood **pulp**'.

After it is mixed with water, the pulp flows onto a screen where the water drains off, leaving a thin wet sheet of pulp.

Big hot rollers press and then dry this wet pulp as it moves along **conveyor belts**. At the end of the line, the dried pulp comes out as giant rolls of paper. These giant rolls are what the paper factories make into the products that you use every day, such as newspapers, paper towels, and the pages of books that you read.

Because we use so much paper, we must be careful how many trees we cut down to make it. Fortunately, nowadays, a lot of used paper can be remade into new paper by **recycling**. You can help save trees by recycling the magazines, newspapers, and other paper that you use in school and at home.

SEARCH LIGHT

Starting with a tree in a forest, arrange these mixed-up steps in the order they should happen in papermaking: (*Start*) tree → chop down tree, dry, peel bark, roll out sheets, cut up wood, press flat, grind into pulp

LEARN MORE! READ THESE ARTICLES…
PINE (VOLUME 10) • PRINTING (VOLUME 2) • RAINFORESTS (VOLUME 1)

In a paper mill like this, the rolls of paper are sometimes as big as the trees they are made from.
© Philip Gould/Corbis

DID YOU KNOW?
According to Chinese historical records, the first paper was made from tree bark, hemp (a plant used to make rope), rags, and fishing nets.

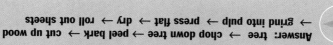

Answer: tree → chop down tree → peel bark → cut up wood → grind into pulp → press flat → dry → roll out sheets

Drawing with Light

The word 'photography' comes from two ancient Greek words: *photo*, for 'light', and *graph*, for 'writing' or 'drawing'.

Photography, the process of taking pictures, requires a camera. But a camera may be any dark lightproof box with a small opening at one end that lets in light. Most cameras have glass **lenses** to help focus the light into the back of the box on the section that holds the film.

Cameras work basically as our eyes do. Light enters the front and shines a picture on the back.

In your eye, light enters through an opening called the 'pupil'. The camera's opening is its aperture. Your iris controls how much light enters your eye. The camera's shutter does the same. In eyes and in most cameras, the light then passes through a lens. In your eye, the picture is

SEARCH LIGHT

Match the parts of the camera to the similar parts of an eye:

1. pupil	a) lens
2. iris	b) film
3. lens	c) shutter
4. retina	d) aperture

produced on the retina, the back lining of the eye. In a camera, the film receives and captures the image.

Photographic film is special material that has been treated with chemicals to make it **sensitive** to light. Light shining on film changes the film's chemical makeup. Depending on how much light shines on each part of the film, different shades or colours result.

Finally, in photography, developing the film creates the photograph. Film that has been exposed to light is processed with chemicals that **fix** the image on special paper.

Today, digital cameras don't use film. Instead, they translate the image into numbers recorded on a disk inside the camera. A personal computer decodes these numbers and displays a picture.

LEARN MORE! READ THESE ARTICLES...
MOTION PICTURES (VOLUME 2) • PAINTING (VOLUME 3)
SIGHT AND SOUND (VOLUME 2)

DID YOU KNOW?
The first photograph - a farmhouse with some fruit trees - was taken in about 1826 by a French inventor, Joseph Nicéphore Niepce.

Gutenberg's Gift

SEARCH LIGHT

Why did Gutenberg make the letters on individual pieces of type face backwards? (Hint: Think about looking at writing in a mirror.)

Before about 550 years ago, very few people owned books. In fact, there weren't many books to own. In those days, most books had to be written out by hand. Some books were printed by using wooden blocks with the letters of an entire page hand-carved into each block. The carved side of the block was dipped in ink and pressed onto paper. Both handwritten and woodblock-printed books took a lot of time, energy, and money. Only rich people could afford to buy them.

Then, in the 1450s, a man in Germany named Johannes Gutenberg had an idea for printing books faster.

First, he produced small blocks of metal with one raised backwards-facing letter on each block. These blocks with their raised letters were called 'type'. He then spelled out words and sentences by lining up the individual pieces of type in holders.

The second part of his invention was the printing press. This was basically a 'bed' in which the lines of type could be laid out to create a page. When he inked the lines of type and then used a large plate to press them against a sheet of paper, lines of words were printed on the paper.

Gutenberg's movable type and printing press, unlike carved woodblocks, meant that he could take his lines apart and reuse the letters. Once he had carved enough sets of individual letters, he didn't have to carve new ones to make new pages.

The Bible was one of the earliest books printed by using Gutenberg's movable type. By 1500 the printing presses of Europe had produced about 6 million books!

LEARN MORE! READ THESE ARTICLES...
BIBLE (VOLUME 5) • BRAILLE (VOLUME 2)
PAPER (VOLUME 2)

DID YOU KNOW?
The Chinese actually invented a kind of movable type 400 years before Gutenberg. But Chinese writing uses thousands of characters and they didn't invent a press, so the invention wasn't a success.

The artist had to imagine Gutenberg and his first page
of print. But the printing press in the background is a
fairly accurate image of what the inventor worked with.

Answer: When the letters face backwards on the blocks, they
come out facing forwards on the paper. Try it yourself!

Guglielmo Marconi, seen here in 1922, received the 1909 Nobel Prize for Physics for his development of a way to send electronic signals without using wires.

SEARCH LIGHT

Fill in the gap: After World War I, radio developed from a two-way communication tool into a popular instrument for _____.

Thank You, Mr Marconi

Before there was television, people got much of their news and entertainment from the radio. And many still do!

Invention of the radio began in 1896 when the Italian scientist Guglielmo Marconi **patented** a wireless **telegraph** process. Marconi knew that energy can travel in invisible waves through the air and that these waves can be captured electronically to send and receive signals. His invention allowed people to send messages to each other over great distances without having to be connected by wires.

A Marconi wireless telegraph set (1912), the 'parent' of the voice-transmitting radio.
© Underwood & Underwood/Corbis

Marconi and others added to his invention, working out how to add sound to these messages to make the first radios. These were used simply for sending and receiving messages. During World War I the armed forces used radios for this purpose. It was after the war that radio became popular as a means of entertainment.

During the 1920s radio stations were set up all over the world. In the early days, most of the radio programmes gave news or **broadcast** lectures and some music. As more and more people started to listen to the radio, more popular entertainment programmes were added. These included comedies, dramas, game shows, mysteries, soap operas, and shows for children.

Radio shows remained very popular until the 1950s. That's when television began to catch on. As it happens, television actually works in the same basic ways that radio does! It uses special equipment to send and receive pictures and sound in the form of electronic signals.

Today, radio **technology** is used in many ways. Cordless telephones, mobile phones, and garage-door openers all use radio technology. And radio entertainment programmes are still going strong.

LEARN MORE! READ THESE ARTICLES...

ECHOES (VOLUME 1) • ELECTRICITY (VOLUME 2) • TELEVISION (VOLUME 2)

Answer: After World War I, radio developed from a two-way communication tool into a popular instrument for entertainment.

From Rafts to Ocean Liners

We don't know exactly how the first transport over water happened. But it's not hard to imagine how it might have come about.

Long ago, people used anything that would float to move things across water, including bundles of reeds, large jars, and covered baskets.

Perhaps one day someone tied three or four logs together and made a raft. Maybe someone else hollowed out a log as a type of **canoe**. These log boats could be moved by people paddling with their hands. Later they might have used a stick or a pole to make their boat move faster.

Whoever put the first sail on a boat made a wonderful discovery. Sailing was faster and easier than paddling because it caught the wind and used it to move the boat.

SEARCH LIGHT

From each pair, pick the boat that was developed first:
a) raft or sailing boat
b) submarine or canoe
c) paddle steamer or rowing boat

Eventually, someone built a ship that used a sail and long paddles, called 'oars'. When there was little or no wind, the sailors rowed with the oars. In time, sailors learned to turn, or 'set', a sail to make the boat go in almost any direction they wanted.

Later, paddles were used in giant wheels that moved large boats through the water. A steam engine powered these paddle wheels, which were too heavy to turn by hand. Steamboats cruised rivers, lakes, and oceans all over the world.

Today, ships and boats use many different types of engine. Most ships use oil to **generate** power. Some submarines run on nuclear power. But on warm days, many people still enjoy travelling on water by paddling, sailing, and even rafting.

LEARN MORE! READ THESE ARTICLES...
FERDINAND MAGELLAN (VOLUME 4)
SUBMARINES (VOLUME 2) • VIKINGS (VOLUME 4)

> **DID YOU KNOW?**
> In 1947 the Norwegian scientist Thor Heyerdahl and a small crew sailed across more than 8,000 kilometres of ocean on a balsawood raft called the *Kon-Tiki*. It was an experiment to see whether ancient Americans could have settled some Pacific islands.

Today's ocean liners are a popular way for people to get from one place to another and have a holiday on the way.
© Corbis

Eyes That Hear, Speech That's Seen

Mary: 'Can you come to the shop with me?'

Sara: 'I'll ask my mother'.

If Mary and Sara were like most girls you know, their conversation would not be unusual. But Mary and Sara are deaf, which means that they can't hear. However, they can understand each other.

How?

Well, one way that people who are deaf communicate is by using sign language. Sign language replaces spoken words with finger and hand movements, **gestures**, and facial expressions. People using sign language can actually talk faster than if they were speaking out loud.

Another way people who are deaf may communicate is through lip-reading. People who lip-read have learned to recognize spoken words by reading the shapes and movements speakers make with their lips, mouths, and tongues. Lip-readers usually speak out loud themselves even though they can't hear what others say.

Deaf child learning to speak using touch, sight, and imitation.
© Nathan Benn/Corbis

Some people who are deaf use hearing aids or cochlear **implants** to help them hear the sounds and words that others hear. (The cochlea is part of the ear.) Hearing aids usually fit outside the ear and make sounds louder. Cochlear implants are inside the ear and use electrical signals to imitate sounds for the brain. Often children and adults with hearing aids or implants have lessons to learn to speak as hearing people do.

There are many schools for children who are deaf or hearing-**impaired**. There they may learn all or some of the skills of lip-reading, sign language, **oral** speech, and the use of hearing aids and implants. Older students may attend Gallaudet University in Washington, D.C., U.S., a university especially for people who are deaf.

LEARN MORE! READ THESE ARTICLES…
BRAILLE (VOLUME 2) • HELEN KELLER (VOLUME 4) • TELEPHONES (VOLUME 2)

Many deaf children learn to communicate by using sign language.
© Mug Shots/Corbis

DID YOU KNOW?
Some famous people have been deaf:
Juliette Gordon Low, who founded the
Girl Scouts; 1995 Miss America
Heather Whitestone; and LeRoy
Colombo, who, as a lifeguard, saved
907 people.

Answer: In addition to lip-reading, sign language allows many deaf
people to communicate. And some deaf people use hearing aids
or implants to help them hear sound and spoken language.

Silent Stalkers
of the Sea

Because they are meant to spend most of their time underwater, submarines are designed and built quite differently from other ships.

Submarines must be airtight so that water can't get inside them when they **submerge**. They also need to have strong **hulls** because the pressure of seawater at great depths is strong enough to crush ships. And submarines need special engines that don't use air when they are underwater. Otherwise, they would quickly run out of air and shut down! So most modern subs are powered by electric batteries when they're submerged. Some are powered by nuclear energy.

Because a submarine is completely closed up, it must have special instruments to act as its eyes and ears underwater. A periscope is a viewing **device** that can be raised up out of the water to allow the submarine officers to see what is around them. Another special system, sonar, 'hears' what is under the water by sending out sound waves that bounce off everything in their path. These echoes send a sound-picture back to the sub.

But why build submarines in the first place? Well, submarines have been very useful in times of war. They can hide underwater and take enemy ships by surprise.

Submarines have peaceful uses too. Scientists use smaller submarines, called 'submersibles', to explore the huge ocean floors and the creatures that live there. People also use submersibles to search for sunken ships and lost treasure. The luxury liner *Titanic* was discovered and explored with a submersible 73 years after it sank in the Atlantic Ocean.

SEARCH LIGHT

Fill in the gaps: Submarines need _____ that don't use up _____.

LEARN MORE! READ THESE ARTICLES...
ECHOES (VOLUME 1) • NUCLEAR ENERGY (VOLUME 2)
JULES VERNE (VOLUME 4)

DID YOU KNOW?
The *Nautilus*, the first nuclear sub, was once caught by a fishing net. The fishing boat and its unhappy crew were towed for several kilometres before the situation was sorted out.

When a submarine travels above the water, officers can stand on top of the conning tower. This is the raised deck of the ship.
© George Hall/Corbis

Answer: Submarines need engines that don't use up air.

Staying in
Touch

The telephone is the most popular communication **device** of all time.

Alexander Graham Bell invented the telephone in 1876. In 11 years there were more than 150,000 telephones in the United States and 26,000 in the United Kingdom. In 2001 there were an estimated 1,400,000,000 telephones worldwide.

Traditional telephones have three main parts: a **transmitter**, a receiver, and a dialler. There is also a switch hook, which hangs up and disconnects the call.

When you speak into the phone, the transmitter changes the sound of your voice into an electrical signal. The transmitter is basically a tiny **microphone** in the mouthpiece. On the other end of the call, the receiver in the listener's earpiece changes that electrical signal back into sound. The receiver is a tiny vibrating disk, and the electrical signal vibrates the disk to make the sounds of the caller's voice.

When you make a call, the phone's dialler sends a series of clicks or tones to a switching office. On a rotating dial phone, dialling the number 3 causes three clicks to interrupt the normal sound on the line (the dial tone). On a touchtone phone, a pushed number interrupts the dial tone with a new sound. These interruptions are a form of code. The telephone exchange 'reads' the code and sends the call to the right telephone receiver.

Since the 1990s, mobile phones have become hugely popular worldwide. Mobile phones connect with small transmitter-receivers that each control an area, or 'cell'. As a person moves from one cell to the next, the mobile phone switches the signal it receives to the new cell.

SEARCH LIGHT

A telephone receiver is a
a) vibrating disk.
b) dial tone.
c) tiny microphone.

LEARN MORE! READ THESE ARTICLES...
ECHOES (VOLUME 1) • ELECTRICITY (VOLUME 2) • RADIO (VOLUME 2)

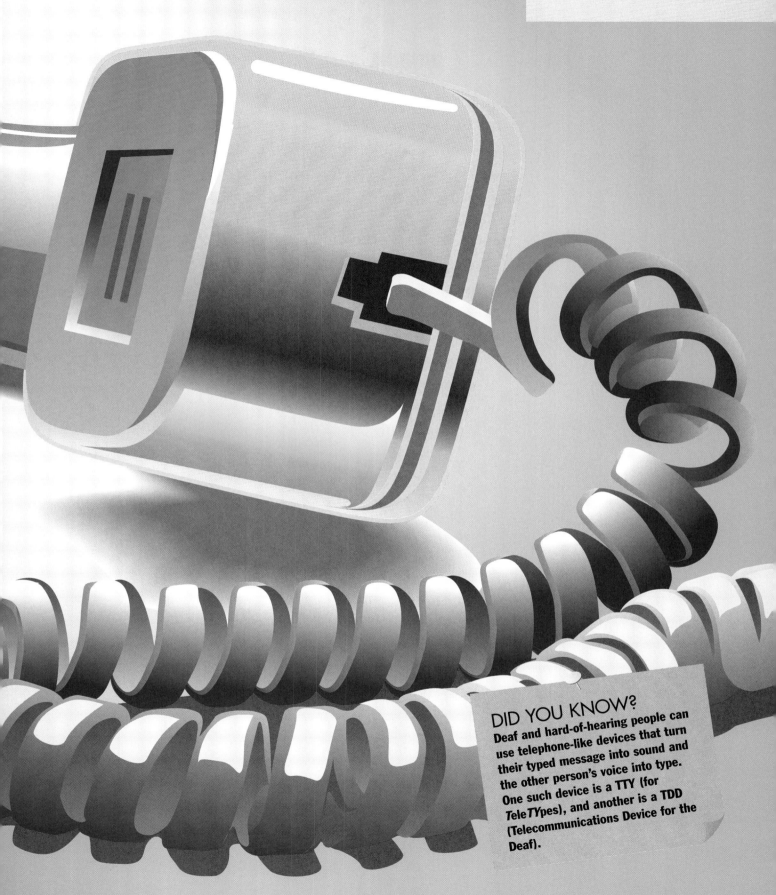

DID YOU KNOW?
Deaf and hard-of-hearing people can use telephone-like devices that turn their typed message into sound and the other person's voice into type. One such device is a TTY (for TeleTYpes), and another is a TDD (Telecommunications Device for the Deaf).

Exploring the Sky

The stars we see in the night sky look like little points of light. But they are vastly larger than they look. Almost all of them are much bigger than our Earth. The stars look tiny because they're very far away. If you rode in the fastest rocket for your entire life, you wouldn't make it even halfway to the closest star.

Fortunately, telescopes let us explore the stars without leaving the Earth.

A simple telescope is tube-shaped and has a special kind of **magnifying** glass, called a '**lens**', at each end. Other telescopes use mirrors or both lenses and mirrors to enlarge the faraway view. Lenses and mirrors gather the light from an object, making it seem brighter and easier to see.

Telescopes make stars and planets seem closer. And telescopes let us see much farther than we normally can. Through a simple telescope you can see the rings of the planet Saturn, as well as galaxies outside our own Milky Way. Giant telescopes on mountaintops can view objects much farther away and see with much greater detail. Their lenses and mirrors are often enormous and therefore enormously powerful.

Some modern telescopes don't even look like the ones most of us might look through. These devices, which must travel into space beyond Earth's atmosphere, can sense light and other **radiation** that's invisible to unaided human eyes. These sensitive instruments, such as the Infrared Space Observatory and the Hubble Space Telescope (pictured here), have shown scientists such wonders as the dust in space between galaxies and the births and deaths of stars.

LEARN MORE! READ THESE ARTICLES...
ASTRONOMY (VOLUME 2) • GALILEO (VOLUME 4) • SATURN (VOLUME 2)

DID YOU KNOW?
Special radio telescopes 'listen' to the radio signals produced by stars, galaxies, and other objects. One group in New Mexico, U.S., includes 27 'dish' antennas spread over 40 kilometres.

SEARCH LIGHT

Find and correct the mistake in the following sentence: Telescopes make faraway objects seem faster than they look with the unaided eye.

Behind the Hubble Space Telescope, you can see the Earth's atmosphere outlined.
NASA

The World in a Box

The British Broadcasting Corporation (BBC) offered the first public television (TV) programming in 1936. But World War II stalled the development and popularity of the new invention.

At first, people preferred radio to the small, fuzzy black and white pictures and poor sound of early TV. Very few people could even receive the programmes. In the United States, when the 1947 World Series of baseball was shown on TV, many Americans watched and afterward decided to buy TV sets. The turning point in Great Britain came with the televised coronation of Queen Elizabeth II in 1953.

The first TV programmes - mostly news reports, comedies, variety shows, soap operas, and dramas - were based on popular radio shows. Gradually, detective programmes, game shows, sports, films, and children's programmes joined the line-up.

In some countries, independent businesses called 'networks' - groups of stations linked together - choose TV programming and make money by selling advertising time. In other countries, people buy a TV and radio licence, which helps pay for government-sponsored programming. Another system, called 'cable TV', often sells subscriptions that allow viewers to watch their shows.

Broadcast TV works much as radio does. Special equipment changes images and sound into electrical signals. These signals are sent through the air and are received by individual **aerials**, which pass the signals on to the TV sets. There they are read and changed back into images and sound.

The TV technology keeps changing. Colour TV became popular in the mid-1960s, and cable TV and videocassette recorders (VCRs) spread during the '80s. Today, advances such as digital videodiscs (DVDs), high-definition TV, and satellite dishes provide even better picture and sound.

Earth-orbiting satellites have improved TV broadcasting. In fact, the only things that haven't changed much are the kinds of shows people watch and enjoy!

LEARN MORE! READ THESE ARTICLES...
JUDI DENCH (VOLUME 3) • RADIO (VOLUME 2) • THEATRE (VOLUME 3)

Big-screen TV and video recording have made the
viewing experience very different from TV's early days.
Now we can watch ourselves on TV!
© Jose Luis Pelaez, Inc./Corbis

DID YOU KNOW?

All the first television shows were live. You saw everything as it was happening, and if people made mistakes, you saw those, too.

Answer: TRUE. Early TV had poor picture and sound quality, and people preferred to listen to radio and use their imaginations.

Before There Were Automobiles

Long ago, most people had to walk wherever they wanted to go on land. Later, when large animals began to be **domesticated,** some people rode on camels, horses, donkeys, oxen, and even elephants.

Then came the discovery of wheels. The people of Mesopotamia (now in Iraq) built wheeled carts nearly 5,000 years ago. But so far the earliest cart that has actually been found is one made later than those in Mesopotamia, by people in ancient Rome. It was simply a flat board. At first, people pulled carts themselves. Later, they trained animals to do this.

As people used more and more carts, they had to make roads on which the carts could travel easily. In Europe and North America, carts developed into great covered wagons and then into stagecoaches. Pulled by four or six fast horses, stagecoaches first bounced and rolled along the roads in the mid-1600s. They became an important method of public transport during the 19th century.

It wasn't until the steam engine was invented that a better means of transportation was developed. This was the railway train. Steam **locomotives** used steam pressure from boiling water to turn their wheels.

The first passenger train service began in England in 1825. Soon trains were carrying hundreds of thousands of people wherever iron tracks were laid.

The first motorcars were not built until the late 1890s. Some of the earliest were made in the United States and England, though they were slow and broke down a lot. They looked much like carts with fancy wheels. What most of us would recognize as a motorcar wouldn't come along for several more years.

LEARN MORE! READ THESE ARTICLES...
AUTOMOBILES (VOLUME 2) • CAMELS (VOLUME 12) • SPACECRAFT (VOLUME 2)

SEARCH LIGHT

What were the first things used by people to get around?
a) their own feet
b) carts
c) donkeys

Answer: a) their own feet

Making Cloth

'**S**hu-dul-ig! Shu-dul-og!'

The shuttle in this weaver's left hand flies back and forth, carrying its thread.

A shuttle is part of a loom, a machine that makes cloth. Cloth is composed of threads crisscrossing each other.

'Warp' threads run up and down lengthwise on the loom. The shuttle carries the 'weft' thread back and forth, passing it over and under the sets of warp thread. This is how simple cloth like muslin is woven. Making patterned and other complicated cloth is a more complex weaving process.

The threads for weaving cloth are made of fibres - thin, wispy strands often tangled together. Some fibres come from animals, some from plants, and some from synthetic (artificial) sources. Fine silk fibres come from the cocoon of a silkworm - actually the caterpillar stage of a moth. People learned to spin fibres into threads a very long time ago.

The most commonly used animal fibre is wool. Most wool is the hair of sheep, but some comes from goats, camels, llamas, and several other animals. Woollen cloth keeps you nice and warm when it's cold outside.

Cotton is a plant fibre. Some cotton fibres are so thin that just about half a kilo of them can be spun into a thread about 160 kilometres long! Work clothing and summer clothes are often made of cotton.

Fine silk cloth is shiny and smooth. It is more expensive than cotton because silkworms need a lot of care. And each silkworm makes only a small amount of silk.

Today, weaving by hand has become mostly a specialized **craft**. As with much other manufacturing, modern cloth is usually produced by machines.

Which of the following descriptions matches the term 'weft'?
a) cross threads
b) up-and-down threads
c) weaving machine
d) source of silk

LEARN MORE! READ THESE ARTICLES...
COMPUTERS (VOLUME 2) • COTTON (VOLUME 10) • SHEEP (VOLUME 12)

DID YOU KNOW?
The strongest piece of weaving anywhere is a spider web. One strand of spider silk is thought to be stronger than an equal-sized piece of steel.

G L O S S A R Y

absorb to soak up

agriculture farming

aerial metallic rod or wire for sending or receiving radio waves or other energy signals

artificial made by human beings rather than occurring in nature

atmosphere the envelope of gases that surrounds a planet

axis imaginary pole going through the centre of the Earth or other heavenly body

bacterium (plural: bacteria) tiny one-celled organism too small to see with the unaided eye

broadcast to send out a programme or message to a group, usually by radio, television, or the Internet

canoe a small, light, and narrow boat having sharp front and back ends and moved by paddling

cartridge sealed container

chemical one of the combined substances making up living and nonliving things

comet chunk of frozen space debris that has a shiny tail and orbits the Sun

convert to change

conveyor belt a loop of material that can move objects from one worker or workstation to the next for the steps needed to make a product

core central part

countless too many to count

craft (noun) a skill or trade; (verb) to make skillfully, usually by hand

crater bowl-shaped dent in a surface

data factual information or details

debris rubbish or fragments

decade ten-year period

device tool or piece of equipment

devise to work out, invent, or plan

diameter the length of a straight line through the centre of an object

domesticate to tame

drawback problem or bad side

dwindle to become smaller or less

economical inexpensive and efficient

edit to cut down to a different or shorter version

element in science, one of the simplest substances that make up all matter

expanse large area

fix in photography, to make an image lasting

fuse an electrical safety device

gear a toothed wheel that works as part of a machine

generate to create or be the cause of

gesture movement of the body, arms, hands, or legs to express feelings or thoughts

glider a soaring aircraft similar to an airplane but without an engine

gravity force that attracts objects to each other, keeps people and objects anchored to the ground, and keeps planets circling the Sun

harness to control, much as an animal may be hitched up and controlled by its harness

hull hard outer shell of a seed or a boat or ship

impaired damaged or limited

imperial having to do with an emperor or empire

implant (noun) object inserted within living tissue; (verb) to insert securely or deeply

indivisible unable to be divided

investigate to look into or study

laboratory place where science tests and experiments are done

lens (plural: lenses) curved piece of glass that concentrates rays of light

locomotive railway vehicle that carries the engine that moves train cars along

lunar having to do with the Moon

magnify to make something appear larger

manufacture to make from raw materials, by hand or by machine

massive heavy or large

matter physical substance or material from which something is made

meteorite a mass of material from space that reaches the Earth's surface

method way or system

microphone a device that changes sound to electrical signals, usually in order to record or send sound

mineral naturally occurring nonliving substance

module independent unit made to be part of a larger structure

molecules the smallest possible pieces of a particular substance

oral having to do with the mouth

orbit (verb) to travel around an object; (noun) an object's path around another object

paraffin fuel for lanterns

paralyse to make someone or something unable to move

particle tiny bit or piece

patent (verb) to legally protect the rights to make, use, or sell an invention; (noun) document that legally protects the ownership and use of an invention

potential possible

propeller a device that uses blades that fan outwards from a central hub to propel (move) a vehicle, such as a boat or an airplane

pulp mashed-up pasty glop; fleshy material of a soft fruit

radiation energy sent out in the form of rays, waves, or particles

ray beam

recycle to pass used or useless material through various changes in order to create new useful products from it

refinery factory that treats crude petroleum and separates it into different parts

ritual a formal custom or ceremony, often religious

rotate to spin or turn

rotation spinning or turning

satellite natural or man-made object that circles another object - usually a planet

scholarship an award of money to help pay for a person's education

sensitive easily affected

solar having to do with the Sun

space shuttle rocket-launched airplane-like vehicle that transports people to and from space

sphere ball or globe

spool reel for winding lengths of materials such as tape, thread, or wire

standard commonly accepted amount or number

storage space to keep or hold on to things

submerge put under water

superior better than

surgery a medical procedure or operation for treating a disease or condition

technology the theories and discoveries of science put into practice in actual actions, machines, and processes

telegraph a device for sending coded messages over long distances by using electrical signals

traditional usual; well known because of custom or longtime use

transmitter a device that sends messages or code

vehicle a device or machine used to carry something